GIRLS ON FILM

JULIE BURCHILL

PANTHEON BOOKS
NEW YORK

PHOTO CREDITS

The author and publisher would like to thank the following for permission to reproduce pictures: **BBC Hulton Picture Library**: 8, 9, 11, 14, 17, 19, 20, 24 (right), 27 (top right), 30 (left), 39 (top right), 56, 58 (right), 68, 69, 71, 77 (top right, bottom), 78, 79 (right), 81 (bottom right), 84, 85 (top), 96 (right), 102, 105, 106, 107, 109 (left), 110, 111, 116 (top), 125, 126 (right), 143, 150, 154, 161 (top), 164, 166, 168 (right), 175, 184 (left); **Kobal Collection**: 34, 81 (top, bottom left), 83, 85 (bottom), 87, 88, 89, 91, 92, 116 (bottom left), 128 (left), 177; **London Features International Ltd**: 64, 75 (left), 77 (top left), 100, 136, 168 (left), 182, 183, 184 (right), 186, 189, 190; **National Film Archive London**: 6, 7, 10, 16, 22, 24 (left), 25, 27 (top left, bottom), 29, 30 (right), 32 (*To Have And Have Not* ©1945 Warner Bros Pictures Inc, ren. 1972 by United Artists TV Inc), 39 (top left, bottom), 41, 42, 45, 47, 50, 53, 54, 58 (left), 61, 67, 75 (right), 79 (left), 95, 96 (left), 99 (bottom), 103, 123 (*Butterfly* ©Universal Pictures, a division of Universal City Studios Inc, courtesy of MCA Publishing Rights, a division of MCA Inc), 124 (top), 126 (left), 127, 128 (right), 129 (courtesy of The Rank Organisation plc), 133 (courtesy of Castle Hill Productions Inc), 145 (courtesy of ABC Pictures International), 152, 158, 161 (bottom), 185; **Rex Features Ltd**: 73, 99 (top), 109 (right, *Mommie Dearest* ©1981 Paramount Pictures Corporation), 116 (bottom right), 119, 120, 124 (bottom), 167.

Library of Congress Cataloging-in-Publication Data
Burchill, Julie.
   Girls on film.
   1. Women in moving-pictures. I. Title.
PN1995.9.W6B87   1986   791.43'028'0922   86-42880
ISBN 0-394-75020-9 (U.S.)

Contents

Introduction

We are encouraged to worship men in life, love, bed, war and politics but we are only encouraged to worship girls on film. Recently, not even this heaven-haven has been available: Cimino, Scorcese and Coppola and the rest of the Boys Town Mafia would prefer us to sit in the darkened mezzanine gasping at the touching relationship between man and man.

In these boy-meets-boy blockbusters there can be no room for the kind of girl who made the cinema great. We have progressed from the days of the 'women's film'. Yet the thirst to see the films of the goddesses, to sniff their underwear at Sotheby's, to remake and remodel their life stories grows more unquenchable every year. They were the stuff that dreams are made of and they were our beasts of burden. Our dreams are too heavy for us to carry alone.

Why do we fall in love in the flea-pit? A certain smile, a cigarette smoked with sass, a fault, a failure, a country of origin, a disguise, a pair of eyes? Whatever it is we aren't getting it from the Vietnam Vets and Italian Stallions of today's big screen. A clue clothed as a stolid statistic: in 1946 there were over 1,500 million admissions to cinemas and in 1980 there were 86 million. Perhaps the women's films were people's films after all.

Chapter One
AND GRIFFITH CREATED GIRL

In the beginning was the American Girl – the squaw, silent by some tepee. Long after she was gone, the white man decided to re-create the American Girl, and she too was silent, on the screen.

She was created by David Wark Griffith, as surely as the moving picture was created by Edison. Film was born at the start of what Frederick Lewis Allen called 'The Big Change', the biggest change in human history – when mankind became mechanized. By 1892 the poor and the young could see moving pictures in the penny arcades, gems like *What The Bootblack Saw* and *How Bridget Served The Salad Undressed*. In 1896 *Fatima* caused vapours at the Chicago World's Fair with her Egyptian shimmy. But even when the moving pictures lengthened into small stories and showed themselves to sit-down audiences, they were despised as a shadowy carbon of the living theatre, scaled down to size and vulgarized for shop-girls and sweatshop boys.

It was despised by men like David Wark Griffith, the son of a Kentucky Confederacy 'hero' whose fortunes were left high and dry on the rocks of the post-Civil War fallen South. Griffith worked as a shop assistant, a hop picker and then, sinking as low as a Southern gentleman could sink, he became an actor with a travelling company. He saw it as a shoddy stop-gap between writing plays and changed his name with shame.

Ten years later, the only success he had had was in the writing of narratives for motion pictures when he was given the chance to become a film director by Biograph. As he prepared, in 1908, to direct *The Adventures Of Dolly* he told his wife, 'In a way it's very nice but, you know, we can't go on for ever and not tell our friends and family how we are earning our living.'

But Griffith's contempt for the motion picture became concern. He tried to breathe life into the stillborn art. He moved cameras from one place to

D.W. Griffith: the creator contemplates public ignorance and the selling power of rewritten history

another. He moved the camera closer to the actors and created the close-up. Biograph officials were shocked by this: the audience would think that the camera was worked by an amateur and that the actors' legs had been cut off accidentally! The camera crept closer and closer over the next four years despite the disgust of the Biograph bigwigs. The audience, meanwhile, which included a large number of Old World immigrants who could barely read sub-titles, were delighted at being able to deduce the plot from the expressions on the faces of the actors. The cinema at last had something of its own. By 1911 his name was David Wark Griffith again.

Close-ups made youth an essential, so Griffith dismissed the old buffoons and gathered around him a posse of pretty teenagers. Mary Pickford and Blanche Sweet had been extras, Mabel Normand a model, Mae Marsh a rabid fan. What they lacked in acting experience they made up for in their eagerness to take orders, registering emotions for the creeping camera

Mary Pickford: pretty teenager

Mae Marsh: bankable blank

under Griffith's instructions – often without knowing the part they played or the plot they took part in.

No sooner was film as a malleable messenger on its feet than the men who shaped it began to bend it to their whim of the moment: to inform the inhabitants of this huge, primitive playpen, this America, of their history – according to the Gospel of Director. Griffith produced *Man's Genesis* in 1912 in which 'Weak Hands' wins out over his callous next-cave neighbour 'Brute Force' by crafting a handy axe. In the same year *Queen Elizabeth* came from France, the title role romped through by Sarah Bernhardt and her wooden leg. In 1913 the Roman epic *Quo Vadis?* arrived from Italy and ran at the Astor for twenty-two weeks at the record admission price of $1.50 before being shown all across America at legitimate theatres. With *Quo Vadis?*, the movies acquired cachet, and a crowd of high-steppers who would not have been seen drunk at the five-cent flicks. It was ironic that, while Old World immigrants whimpered and wept their way through all-American melodrama, the cream of American society cheered the chariot races on loan from Europe. Already the cinema was providing that which mankind began to crave the moment he became conscious – the 'Other'.

The eternal American dilemma gripped Griffith – the pioneer made to feel an upstart. He searched his cerebral souvenirs for some story, some epic episode in America's history that could save the New World's honour. As the son of 'Roaring Jake' Griffith he needed to look no further than

Sarah Bernhardt: but burned harder B.C. (Before Celluloid)

the legendary lies that the Southlands and their soft-spoken ghosts had cherished and burnished for three generations.

The Clansman, by the Reverend Thomas E. Dixon, another Southerner, had enjoyed success as a book and a play for years. He and Griffith worked like two black-eyed peas in a pod on the screenplay and when it was finished they decided that it was too panoramic to be limited to the Ku Klux Kult end of the market. Instead, the whole country was lured into the conspiracy and the cinema by the mothering, smothering title, *Birth Of A Nation*.

Birth Of A Nation is an impressive film – if one can suspend one's brain-power right through its tortuous duration and believe that the freed Negro is inevitably a cross between an anarchist and an animal while the Southern woman is unimpeachably an angel in taffeta and human disguise. This theory is made especially hard to take when Southern sainthood is personified in the poisonous sweetness of Lillian Gish, every inch the smarmy charmer who'd get a monumental kick out of setting up a sub-human ex-slave on a sex assault charge. When Gish leads the Klan's horse-back procession after her 'rescue' from rapacious Negroes, her delicate hand on the belt of the leading Hood, her precious frail body, so newly-saved and Born Again, shrouded in white, she is Griffith's vision of impenetrable America, stronger than Britannia, braver than Jeanne d'Arc,

Lillian Gish: pretty poison

more beautiful than any mere *mortal* (or Northern) woman could ever be, with all of history and hope for the future in her eyes. She is above all *dangerous*; she is an ideal that many American women will go mad trying to live up to and that many American men will commit atrocities for, in this misguided crusade to protect her from anything 'Other'. Later she may have a permanent wave and change her name to Doris Day – who knows?

The storm caused by this celluloid manifesto soaked Wall Street and swept away the White House on a tide of praise. Money and power, which translates into American as 'moribund', loved it precisely because of the evil that A.E. Pillsbury recoiled from: 'It gambles on the public ignorance of our own history.' From the year of their 'Birth' to 1927, the Ku Klux Klan, revived and rampant, fully believed that Griffith was a card-carrying, cross-burning comrade in his wildest dreams, and this is one point on which the geeks and I agree.

Let us leave Mr Griffith here, then, rambling through the Taras of his aesthetically astute semi-insanity, peering under the bed like the legendary Southern spinster for that big black buck, watching with God-fearing glee as white wings sprout on the back of the nearest available Southern girl. We should thank him, though, for the gift of the Face which actors wear like a badge of courage and which, if the huddled masses can read into it whatever they lack, will turn the actor into a star.

11

Chapter Two
FROM WIMP TO VAMP AND BACK AGAIN

It was built as a town but it served as an analyst's couch. Instead of a certificate of psychiatry framed and mounted on the wall there was the sign set in the hills. If the British are a nation of shopkeepers then the Americans are a nation of shrinks and madmen.

Immediately America became conscious that the rest of the world was looking at it, it began to shout loudly that it was *not* the ashtray of the planet, that its people were *not* dog-ends; rather, they were God's Chosen. *American*. It stopped being a nationality and became a manifesto.

Griffith and his partner-in-neurosis Cecil B. DeMille invented a big evil world in which the good guys, the potential Americans, had been called to the untamed continent by their Maker. (One could view America today as a sort of Good Guys' Convention that has lasted two hundred years.) The men who controlled the Dream Machine had to control history in order to calm their screaming souls, they had to defuse the massive disorder of this huge country made up of a spectrum of climates and terrain and peoples which had been told to get on with the business of being a sovereign territory just like a real roots country, a France or a Japan. By making sense of history, cutting it down to size, the Dream Merchants could harness the hysteria that in America always seems about to boil over and coat the country in the lava of carnage.

Better still, they would *revise* history – stick in a few broads and some human interest and sell it as a side-show. Familiarity would breed contempt in the American public and the task of pulling together a country out of a million patchwork scraps would not seem so awesome after all.

There were two cinematic modes of promoting Americanism as a valid theory of evolution. There was the straightforward (or backward) historical opus, the Bible via the Gospel of Saint Cecil, which proved conclusively that every society which had existed before AMERICA had crumbled because it was not AMERICAN. Un-Americanism was a big aesthetic force in epics and other titillations because it was a clever way to squeeze past Mr Censor; so long as the participating actors were not portraying Americans, you could throw in slavery, polygamy, flagellation, mayhem, murder, concubinage, greed, lust and the good old-fashioned downfall of civilization. Epics were also a good boost for the capitalist fight against Communism. DeMille could go in for that good old American indoor sport, the re-writing of history, by showing that all world events, all downfalls of societies had happened because of the perfidy of one woman or the predilections of one potentate – not because of the conflict between oppressed and oppressor.

Thus America was glorified by the bad behaviour of other naughty nations. On a more positive and picturesque level, America was glorified by moving pictures that threw out the wholesomeness and happiness of the contemporary American like balm over the trusting audience. As psychiatrists constantly harp back to the sex habits of their parents, so the kind of woman that this mixed-up country on the couch craved is significant. As its first sweetheart, this country founded on genocide must have someone pure and blameless, someone whose lily-white soul could suck out all the poison guilt and leave the nation feeling good about itself. This was the function that the first real star – and by star I mean someone who *was* her films, and who had the box-office power to blackmail her biggers and betters – Mary Pickford, America's Sweetheart, performed, as gently and efficiently as a nurse giving a blanket-bath.

Like the second star of the American cinema, Charlie Chaplin, who arrived soon after her and against whom from 1914 to 1918, her peak years, she measured her salary, demanding and receiving a colossal rise every time Chaplin received one (as well as being America's first Sweetheart, Pickford was also the first American woman to put equal pay theory into practice), Mary Pickford was dirt poor and determined to be filthy rich. Drilled by her mother since diapers to use her looks as a stepladder to the finer things – dollar bills – of life, born with the typical white-trash name of Gladys Smith but the atypical white-trash face of Miss Muffet or some other nursery rhyme heroine, Mary Pickford looked like the antithesis of what she was. After two years' work for Adolph Zukor she said, 'You know, Mr Zukor, for years I've dreamed of making twenty thousand dollars a year before I was twenty. And I'll be twenty very soon now.' That was Mary Pickford's way of working and winning; before long she was earning half a million dollars a year for suffering, simpering and sunshining her way through a succession of warm baths made celluloid.

Girls changed their names to Blanche Sweet, Arline Pretty and even Louise Lovely in a bid to become the kind of kindergarten cutie in whose mouth money wouldn't melt. But somewhere in Hollywood another extra from the mid-West – Sin City Cincinnati, to be exact – was changing, with the help of a team of power-mad publicity boys, into another kind of girl altogether – a girl literally and purposely the exact opposite of the Pickford posse. A girl to be the female equivalent of the Anti-Christ; the Anti-Madonna. For the first time since Fatima had shimmied silently in Chicago, sex raised its head on screen. And what an ugly head it was! – Theda Bara, who looked like the Loch Ness Monster in a ton of mascara. Although she was a good Jewish-American girl, she was said to be French-Egyptian so that men would not feel they were soiling a hallowed American Miss when they called her rude names in locker rooms. She represented the dirty Old World of sex and, like DeMille's disaster epics, her function was to make America's future look even brighter.

A Fool There Was, the name of the film that shot her to success, more or less describes poor Theodosia Goodman herself. The publicity boys went to town on the raw meat, the red meat, the soul and soil of the sex seeker. The farcicality of her persona makes Feydeau look poker-faced. She was said to be a seeress. She was forced to give interviews in black velvet rooms with incense burning – when she was sure that the last press person had left she would rush to the window and hang out of it. 'Give me AIR!' she would gasp. She was photographed with skeletons (her victims?) and snakes (her

Theda Bara: the unacceptable face of sex

14

playmates?). She crept around looking as swarthy and Un-American as possible so that the sensitive cinema-goer could entertain thoughts of sex without incriminating American Mom and thinking about what she must have done (and perhaps, horror of horrors, still did!) in the dark with American Dad. She made forty films in four years and after the completion of her contract in 1919 waited for further offers. They never came and she never got over the shock. Although Bara married money, she advertised herself as being 'at liberty' in the Hollywood casting directory until her death in 1955.

Although her career was the first sex farce without a punch-line, Theda Bara did perform one magnificent feat for picture-going mankind. She saw active service as the first VAMP (Adventuress – v.t. Attract as vamp, allure, entice – abbrev. of vampire). She had given the American public a taste for bitter Other instead of sweet Dream. Although she was an ugly grub, there could have been no Red Admirals or Painted Ladies, no Ava Gardners or Lana Turners without her.

The vamp was dark, even if Bacall Blonde or Rita Redhead. She came from a non-WASP swamp, pre-industrial, pre-plaything. She was a beautifully coiffed cave-girl. No matter how much lipstick she wore or how marcelled her hair was there was something essentially of nature about her, about her demands and devastation. Her interest in money was purely for want of anything better; when she glimpsed a soulmate she would jilt the billionaire and run across a continent to claim him. The vamp was compelled by sex and soul, not cents or sense – she snubbed kings to go like a sulky sleepwalker to a handsome, lonesome Joe. She could be a bastard with the boys but basically her patron saint was Saint Francis; men were dumb animals and she, on the whole, was good to them.

The vamp is champ; the very best kind of girl. The vamp was a beacon and a blessing in the cinema, the apex of what a woman on the screen can be. The vamp was beautiful and strong; she made helplessness, which previously and ever since has been the desirable norm for girls on film, look insipid and uninspiring. She came from nowhere and she walked alone. The vamp was a rhapsody and a revolution.

But for the moment the vamp was 'resting'. Until beauty came in to give the vamp the kiss of life, vampism was somewhat worthy of ridicule. It was suddenly a post-War world and thus a new world. Bara, by merely insinuating that she would sleep with a man, could thrill, the territory was so unexplored. Beauty was not a necessity and Bara's imitators, such as Louise Glaum and Valeska Suratt, leapt the hurdle of their plainness by simply pantomiming passion. But now American men had seen beautiful European girls and they expected the same selling-point from their film stars. They got it, too. In the boldness that follows any war, morals took a nosedive and the prettier sort of American girl, who previously would have hooked the hometown hero toot sweet, ran away to be in motion pictures instead.

The movies came to a compromise, defending the chastity of the American girl, while admitting that the Baras and Pickfords must look ridiculous to men who had been at war and experienced girls who had survived hardship without simpering or swatting men like flies. They compromised by creating a girl who could take a man's mind off things but with a wisecrack rather than a waspy-waisted corset, a girl who combined the cuteness of a good girl with the desires of a bad girl. She was Clara Bow – the It Girl, the Brooklyn Bonfire, the Jazz Baby, the Baby Vamp.

A cross between a tomboy and a temptress, Bow's most striking feature was her confidence. She reigned from 1922 to 1930 and she mirrored the American ego at its most thick-skinned. Although America lost one-fiftieth of proportionate British losses in the First World War, they had had the glory of seeming to decide the issue and bringing the War to a close. They went in late and came out rich, as they would do in the next World War, while France and Britain came out destitute. Similarly, Clara Bow smoked in the street, got home late and generally went to the bad but somehow she only had to smile and roll her eyes and all would be forgiven.

Flaming Youth brought her twenty thousand letters and a host of imitators – Jacqueline Logan, Alice White, Sally O'Neil, Phyllis Haver. Their plain names echo with post-War egalitarianism, with the demands of

Shimmied to a standstill: *Flaming Youth*

Clara Bow: the Jazz Baby face that launched a thousand lips

newly-demobbed cannon fodder for film stars who are regular guys rather than snooty tragedy queens or simpering dimwits in need of rescue from rampant Negroes. On the contrary, there was for the first time a Negro influence (as opposed to a Negro problem) on the screen. Girls danced the Charleston and swooned to wailing jazz. The make-up fad of the moment was the 'bee-stung' pout, which looks to me like a child's approximation of a Negro mouth. The largest screen bee-sting ever belonged to Dorothy Mackaill, though Mae Marsh claimed copyright. Twenties films were one long wild party, fuelled on jazz, gin and gasoline, and everyone must dance, even those with two left feet or great acting ability – Joan Crawford, and even Louise Brooks with the face full of doom, later to find fame and ruin in dark, dark Thirties Europe.

It was in the Twenties that European girls began to arrive in Hollywood; in 1915 they might have found big fame as authentic foreign vamps, but by the Twenties the Jazz Baby had absorbed so much of the vamp's autonomy that there really wasn't much of a career in vamping proper. Instead, Alla Nazimova from the Crimea, Vilma Banky from Hungary and Pola Negri from Germany were used to counter Clara Bow's vitality, representing fatigued, fagged-out old Europe in several silents and keeping their best shots for the art of publicity, forever walking a leopard on a chain up Sunset Boulevard in search of a camera shutter.

As the wild party wound down, men worked in laboratories to invent the art of language. Every famous face was furrowed. At each new watershed, it was whispered, the old stars were thrown out like spent champagne bottles. Griffith's unmarked teenagers had replaced the established ex-stage strutters with the advent of the close-up, and obviously a batch of actors whose art was limited to eye-rolling and arm-waving would not translate well into the world of mouth-to-mouth emotion. A new race of post-partying actors were needed, actors who could speak and make people listen, actors whose every articulated thought did not revolve around jalopies and jazz bands. The strong and non-silent type. In 1926 the ambassador and apex of the new breed arrived in Hollywood. Although she had been a silent actress in stark Scandinavia, she acted with her face and her walk, not her hands and hysteria. When speech arrived it was inevitable that films could at last look inward, into the emotions, rather than stay on the surface social whirl, and her face was a road-map of the emotions.

She was the personification of the Other that Bara had lunged at, she was the lure of the Pure that Pickford had dribbled after. She was the mystery that American boy could not find in American girl. She was the perfect stranger, the perfect foreigner – she was Garbo, the first woman.

Garbo was the first European who wasn't interested in making up a title or a tall tale to stun the stupid Americans with. She fought shy of publicity,

Garbo: the girl from Burbank-on-Olympus

which was confidence of the most shocking kind. I am enough, she said. I need no modern marketing. Someone like me travels like wildfire, by word of mouth, handed down like oral history and folklore. She was simply the first beauty in films, and changed the looks of women everywhere. Her fine-featured face, which looked as though it had been worked out with grids and slide-rules, made the American film stars look coarse and un-worthy of worship. Thin was in. Clara Bow was suddenly seen to have thighs like young saplings. The effect was of parading a beautiful whippet alongside a batch of cheap and cheerful mongrels; it might be nice to have a loving little mongrel waiting at home with your slippers, but when you paid the price of entry to a dog show you wanted to see something worth whistling for. (While we're walking the dog metaphors, it was said in 1929 Hollywood that only two stars were so much *themselves*, and sufficient that way, that they were not required by their studios to take singing or dancing lessons – Garbo and Rin-Tin-Tin.)

Garbo's net was wide and her aim was true. She was the first film star to be taken seriously; men who had no use for the movies only had eyes and pens for her mask of tragedy. She suffered – therefore she was! In the Twenties, *Vogue*, which was an awful snob, had bitched 'Phew! Pretty Hollywood!' when it saw anything it considered vulgar. By the Thirties they were trying to make their models look like film stars, photographed in white satin evening gowns sitting on sofas by idle glass bowls of white tulips and lit from the side.

Garbo popularized make-up through beautiful and discreet use of it; she was the first woman who did not use make-up to make herself look like a cartoon character or a clown. Make-up artists decided that you could not just smear mascara and lipstick onto a face like Garbo's like mud on an adobe wall, as had been the case with Bara and Bow; make-up was used to etch even deeper the beautiful peaks and valleys of her face, and was thus popularized amongst girls other than the call variety. In 1931, 1,500 lipsticks were being sold for every *one* sold ten years previously.

The word was 'glamour' – a mixture of gloom and amour to me, 'magic, enchantment, and necromancy' to the dictionary, 'a sort of suffering look' to an unidentified studio head. Whatever it was, Garbo had carried the vital virus from Sweden with her, and it is amusing to see the faces of her contemporaries *before* their studios groomed them as rivals and after. Marlene Dietrich, Joyce Compton, Anna Sten and Tallulah Bankhead – before Garbo, smiling, curled and ready to do your bidding. After Garbo, eyes staring off at impossible vistas, cheekbones that back teeth had been tugged out and tossed away for, the faces of femmes fatalistic.

Apart from being a model for starlets, she was a mirror for the people. It is no coincidence that Garbo rose to fame, suffering and surviving and dying, as the Depression dug its claws into the souls of the working class.

Tallulah Bankhead: before...   ...and after Garbo

Capitalism was having one of its recurring tired and emotional dizzy spells and was a long way from picking up its bed and walking. As the Depression was universal, so her appeal was universal: drunken British men sang 'I Dreamed I Kissed Greta Garbo'; drunken Germans sang 'Du Bist Mein, Greta Garbo'. In France, during the showing of a Garbo film, a spectator walked *over* rows of seats and people, arms raised imploringly, and walked into and *through* the screen. On the North-West Frontier a tribe of warlike Pathan Indians rode down from the hills to see the legendary white woman perform in *Grand Hotel*; when refused admission they opened fire on the cinema.

The sad people loved her but the scared people loathed her. She made sex look something seriously beautiful. Clara Bow might have smoked and stayed out past the stroke of midnight, but she had defused it with humour. Who could do *it* while laughing? The only thing that mollified the guardians of American morals was that Garbo was a foreigner, and what were other countries there for but to make America look morally superior? And it didn't stop there: America caught sex from Garbo. Suddenly flesh was everywhere – in 1933 Sally Blane's creamy thighs above fish-net stockings in *Grand Slam*, Mary Doran's 1932 cami-knickers in *Breach Of Promise*, Joan Crawford and Wallace Beery in *Grand Hotel* in 1932 (one of Garbo's greatest starring vehicles; here was proof that good American Joan had caught sex appeal by contact with the sinful Swede!) sitting on his bed, holding her garter between them like a particularly luscious strand of spaghetti. The Depression gave the studios a social justification for showing girls as less than angels too; being a vamp had once been a vocation or a dare, but now it was something that poor little poor girls were being *driven* into.

This could not be tolerated; in 1927 the Code of the Motion Picture Industry, a gentleman's agreement and therefore no agreement worth whistling for, had been drawn up between the churches and the studios to regulate raunchiness. America, which is always knocking itself out screaming about being a democracy, could not bring itself to admit the fact of a censor. The civic leaders watched with horror at Garbo's portrayal of the Pied Piper of Sex but were helpless; their 'respectable' viewpoint was deeply discredited in the eyes of the American proletariat as they wrote fanmail from the poverty line to these goddesses of the people.

Then in 1933 Franklin Delano Roosevelt introduced the socialist crutch which would prop up crippled capitalism: the New Deal. As people began to recover from the hunger of the Depression years, they felt less ill will towards authority. The churches were the first to act; in 1933 the Episcopal Committee on Motion Pictures denounced the American motion picture as promoting immorality. Catholic bishops formed the National League of Decency, reviewing all films before release and classifying them under

Joan Crawford contemplates the lure of horizontal mobility in *Grand Hotel*

the headings PASSED, OBJECTIONABLE IN PART and CONDEMNED. The findings were announced from the pulpits and the communicants were told that attendance at condemned films constituted a venial sin. In the big cities, which all held large Irish and Italian communities, box-office receipts decreased drastically.

The studios conceded. But they knew that the audiences would not welcome a complete return to the chastity belt. Instead, sex was tampered with like a time-bomb and the vamp was made safe – or as safe as she could be. One new variation was the Wife as Vamp, mockingly vamping only one man. Myrna Loy as Nora Charles made a great and graceful living vamping William Powell as Nick Charles all through the *Thin Man* films of the Thirties. Or there was the vamp who died for her sins; increasingly audiences responded favourably to seeing Garbo die. The American audience had become schizoid about Garbo as her mystery increased rather than decreased with the years, as one always is about a love object one cannot have. I want you but I can't have you so I want you dead! Garbo was Vamp as Deity, and sometimes she was as near as America ever came to a spiritual experience; she was history, she was Mother, she was all-seeing Other. When she vamped, she was increasingly whamped for her sins. She began to die, time and time again, beautifully.

As foreign epics had done, Garbo had attracted high-stepping highbrows to the cinema, but sadly there are not too many highbrows in America. By the time of her greatest artistic triumph, *Camille* in 1936, her films had stopped making money due to her insistence on the best of casts, sets and directors and a salary of $250,000 before the camera started turning. Only her immense popularity in still-Depressed Europe compensated her studio.

In America, to the poorest people who had loved her, she was a reminder of bad old days, angst and anxiety, their beloved country nearly torn apart by its own hunger. There was the shadow of the twentieth century's greatest horror already falling out all over Europe while America was busy forming America First Committees to keep the beloved country out of a European war that was nothing to do with them (America as the Ark, and God about to destroy the unrighteous of the Old World as demonstrated by Cecil B. DeMille?). They needed laughter, laughter loud enough to drown out the screams and the Sieg Heils. They needed the Laughing Vamps, blonde, brilliant and optimistic – everything America wanted to see itself as.

There was Carole Lombard, the only classically beautiful girl ever to make an ass of herself eagerly. Lombard's appeal was that she looked like the kind of girl who would tread on your toe while getting out of her car in front of her Park Avenue apartment building and never even notice you while she behaved like the legendary ugliest girl at the local dance who

Mae West: the life jacket most drowning men would prefer to clutch at

Carole Lombard: put the sex into screwball

would go outside and drink beer in the back seat of a car just because she wanted to be liked. She made Thirties flesh of Zelda Fitzgerald's Twenties manifesto – 'What The Hell!'

Mae West made it onto celluloid just before the New Deal and the Spring Clean, which was just as well, since she got rich and rewarded from vamping rather than reformed. In films like *Diamond Lil* and songs like 'I Like A Man Who Takes His Time' suggestiveness came as easy as breathing – or rather, heavy breathing – to her. She was a scandal – Mary Pickford complained, 'I passed the door of my young niece's room – she's only seventeen and been raised, oh, so carefully – and I heard her singing bits of that song from "Diamond Lil" – I say "that song" just because I'd blush to quote the title.' The scandal was ostensibly just a straight sex complaint but I believe there was more to it than this: the world had lived through Bara and Bow and Garbo, and civilization had not crumbled. Mae West was obviously an *older woman*, and as such should have been Mother material; instead she was seducing young boys and old men. She was in fact forty when she made her first film *Night After Night* in 1932, even older than she looked. She was not young or foreign; she was not dazzled by dollars or desire; she conducted her horizontal business affairs like a very good driver negotiating a hairpin bend. Not only did she speak risqué one-liners like 'It's not the men in my life that count – it's the life in my men,' but she

24

actually *wrote* them. That the vamp could be more than a ventriloquist's dummy must have given the guardians of public morals a whole season of sleepless nights.

But the best of the Laughing Vamps was Jean Harlow. 1930 was a good year for vamps; Garbo spoke, Dietrich arrived and Jean Harlow starred in *Hell's Angels*. She was nineteen. She played working-class girls tackling the mountain of the middle class, popular in the New Deal and Depression days both, as were most gutsy and gorgeous broads. She was urban – no earthbound milkmaid-martyr. She looked like a worker, a glamorous factory girl, sturdy and stroppy – her feet on the ground and her head in *Photoplay*. In fact, she was a dentist's daughter and like that other famous dentist's brat, James Dean, she escaped her solid middle-class roots by playing the depraved deprived.

She had 'tell that to the Marines' eyebrows and a face full of fun, a face that bad things (a husband who committed suicide because of his impotence, a mother who touted her to gangsters) should never have happened to. She played good bad girl, bad good girl, lover and loser; she had a happy film career. She was thought to be not only beautiful but a good actress and an even better comedienne. She got all the best lines and was liked by all the best critics. As her film career progressed, and she grew to look more and more like a big friendly peasant all gussied up for a night

Jean Harlow: Laughing Vamp

out, they called her 'amazing', 'increasingly delightful', 'increasingly astonishing'.

She only began to look serious in *Reckless*, her first film with dapper and dreary William Powell. She fell in love with him and after that she always looked sad, even – especially – when she was smiling. All at once she lost her peasant prettiness and became the tragic, magical beauty we remember.

By the time she made *Saratoga* in 1937 she was not only sad but sick. It was her sixth film with Gable, who looked happy as ever – he always seemed to love playing opposite Harlow, whereas his acting style elsewhere is best described as beatifically bored rigid. When they had sparred in *Red Dust*, *Time* magazine commented on Harlow and Gable's 'curiously similar good-natured toughness' – it was gone from Harlow now and she was pink and new, too tender to touch. William Powell was reluctant to marry her and she was reluctant to live.

She died before *Saratoga* was released. The mother she adored, after whom she had called herself Jean Harlow, refused to call a doctor to her because of her Christian Science principles. This high-principled Jean Harlow Senior was the same woman who once encouraged her daughter to mix with and be mauled by underworld bootleggers and other slobs, simply so that *she* could keep well in with her gangster lover who was impressed by her film star daughter. So Jean Harlow – 'The Baby' as her friends and colleagues called her – turned black and died of uremic poisoning. She was twenty-six. The Laughing Vamp didn't seem quite so funny any more and would soon become serious again. And lovely little Jean Harlow had plotted the path that others – one other lovely, lost-too-soon girl in particular – would follow. Be blonde, be beautiful and be lonely, with the love of the Western World to look back on and only death to look forward to. Before eyes were dry from this American Tragedy, ears were being held to radios to find out how long the tragedy of the world could be held at arm's length. *Fortune* magazine reported that 79 per cent of the population preferred to listen to the radio rather than go to the cinema. To tempt them, picture houses began to give *dishes* to female movie-goers! David Selznick, producer, went one better: he offered them the part of Scarlett O'Hara in the Civil War epic he was hatching – *Gone With The Wind*. It seemed as though every American female between the ages of six and sixty was screen-tested before the part went to the English actress Vivien Leigh – who looked like Hedy Lamarr via Cheltenham Ladies College (Hedy Lamarr, the staggeringly beautiful Hungarian, had made her Hollywood debut in 1938 with *Algiers*, which was notorious for the steamy invitation to 'Come with me to the Casbah!' Lamarr had glamour as Garbo had had it: the ability to stare off into space and seem as though she was thinking about the human dilemma when she was probably just wondering if

Above

Harlow: bending over backwards to be nice to Gable

Above right

Gable and Leigh conduct a little civil sex war in *Gone With The Wind*

Right

Algiers: Charles Boyer offers the Casbah, Hedy wonders whether her toenails need cutting

her toenails needed cutting tonight). It was an unenviable role and there was little anyone could do with it; one felt sympathy for Leigh as she pranced across the screen simpering like a crazy thing. Later, seeing her in other roles, roles that could have been *something*, you realize that she plays everything as she played Scarlett – as a haywire, hysterical ham.

Know-nothings (mostly of the male variety) have called Scarlett O'Hara the most important female role of the Thirties when in fact it is one of the most disposable and uncharacteristic. Leigh won her Oscar but she never won an audience. Those were reserved for women who came to fruition in the decade as strong, struggling contemporary women, not simpering minxes – the Crawfords and Davises who were considered not insipid enough for the part of Scarlett.

O'Hara is a bossy sort of rich girl – the kind they call 'Southern Belles', which so far as I can see means being intolerably rude to Negroes and gazing at any available man as though he was the Eighth Wonder of the World – who plays with fiery Clark Gable and gets taken down a peg or two. The only line of dialogue that rings true from Gable is the one about not giving a damn; he always loathed the film and you can see why. Playing opposite a girl like Leigh, so precious and pleased with herself, while he was living with Lombard and mourning Harlow, must have seemed purgatory.

He might also have been thinking about the real War, which he was soon to volunteer for, and might have despised the trouble taken to burn a fake Atlanta while America could not even take the trouble to burn a few real Nazis. It cannot be a coincidence that while the Second World War was wreaking havoc, America made its second Civil War epic. It was Griffith all over again, except this time the excuse was more expensive – three years, thirteen writers and four million dollars to create three and three-quarter hours of the most boring celluloid ever to be shown on the screen – and America was saying through Hollywood, its translator, 'We've had our war. Leave us alone.'

Scarlett fever aside, the Thirties were an actress's El Dorado, a gold rush – every studio lot was paved with gold so long as you were a good-looking girl. Garbo, Harlow, Hedy, Bette, West, Hepburn, Claudette Colbert as Cleopatra, Carole Lombard, Joan Crawford, Marlene Dietrich – it was in the Thirties that the clout which female stars had had since Mary Pickford blushingly bludgeoned Mr Zukor into putting his hand in his pocket came to be seen on the screen. From Harlow pushing and pulling her hapless husbands to Crawford mowing down men as she scaled the mountain of money and power lying down – women were strong and wayward and the American male, mentally healthy under Roosevelt's rule, had no objections so long as the victorious vamp was handsome.

Behind every great woman there was George Cukor, and this decade of female celluloid supremacy came to a colossal climax with his 1939 film *The*

The Women: the monstrous regiment go into battle

Women. Norma Shearer, Joan Crawford, Rosalind Russell and Paulette Goddard prove conclusively that sarcasm is the highest form of humour – and that men are totally superfluous to a good Thirties film. No men appear here; they are dished about, stolen, spurned and shared but they are never actively *needed*. The only men an actress needed in the Thirties were Cukor to direct her films, Adrian to design her clothes, and someone who looked sweet in uniform to drive her car.

War was raging in Europe by now, and the Forties were familiar, but America was still facing up to the Nazis with all the eagerness and enthusiasm of a dead sloth on its way to the dentist. When America was finally forced to fight by the Japanese, the first casualties were the people of Pearl Harbour and Greta Garbo's career. When the War cut off her precious European market she left movies at the peak of her beauty rather than do smaller films for smaller fees. She had died many times on screen but now she really was gone – the Vamp is dead, long live the Vamp!

Garbo's first beneficiary was her old vamping rival, Marlene Dietrich, who over the War years turned from a symbol of Old World decadence and gender confusion (when she first appeared in a man's suit Paris booed her – then copied her) to a glowing example of the healing power of Americanism. In contrast to Garbo's cold shoulder, Dietrich threw herself, cheekbones and all, onto the Allied side. She had even shown foresight, becoming

29

Marlene Dietrich: from erogenous zones
to battle zones – Vamp as Champ

Betty Grable: the girl with the million
dollar legs – the rest wasn't bad either

an American citizen when Britain went to war in 1939. Her sister was put
into a concentration camp; the German press announced that frequent
contact with Jews rendered Dietrich 'entirely un-German'. In 1943 she
found herself in North Africa and for a solid three years worked at barely
anything but troop concerts. As late as 1975 she was using an introduction
to 'Lili Marlene' that indicates how far the celebrated legs had carried her
in the cause of war work – 'the only important thing I have ever done':
'Now here's a song that is very close to my heart. I sang it during the War, I
sang it for three long years; all through Africa, Sicily, Italy; through Alaska,
Greenland, Iceland; through England, through France, through Belgium
and Holland, through Germany and into Czechoslovakia...'

It was the cementing of the Dietrich Legend, and it gave her the strength
that would eventually allow her to be every inch Dietrich simply by standing on stage, without needing the added magnification of the big screen.
But film stars were still needed – the vamp was addictive and the lack of
flow from war-torn Europe meant America must make its own: girls a cross
between a sister and a siren, a friend and a foreigner.

Men were at war, though, and a new kind of vamp was needed – the
Mascot Vamp. She looked good in a swimsuit; she sometimes smiled. She
might give you a bit of trouble, lead you a merry dance but you'd win in the
end, just like you'd win the War. You didn't need a girl who insisted that
you should be willing to lay down your life for her, though, no Bara or

Garbo melodramas – men were laying down their lives for more important things right now. No, the Mascot Vamps were like poor people's food – spicy, cheap and cheerful and going a long way.

It was now, with the newspapers full of the carnage of war, that the studios set up their girl-grooming machines in earnest. Pictures of pretty girls were at a premium as the papers and magazines attempted to boost the morale of somewhat badly trained servicemen still trying to get used to handling gelignite rather than jelly beans. The studios would groom girls and then throw their photographs at any publication with a circulation larger than ten and wait for feedback. They were photographed on picnics, in sweaters, on staircases, in swimming costumes, but always on show.

One of the chosen cheesecakes – Betty Grable – stayed at this stage and will always be best remembered for the white swimsuit, the long legs and the smile sent from American to American over the warm shoulder. Beneath her glossy blondeness, Grable was plain, and her very plainness made her a nice girl, the kind of girl worth fighting for. Above all she is confidence, she had the ring of confidence before the toothpaste manufacturers ever heard of It, and to the GI this confidence was as oxygen to a deep-sea diver.

Betty Grable was a Fox star, and Fox stars, if they were beautiful or blonde or both, were expected only to stand there and look happy, as Norma Jean will discover to her horror. MGM, home of Garbo, and Columbia, home of Swanson, were accustomed to building faces and bodies into fluid, moving idols and when two young starlets called Julia Turner and Margarita Carmen Cansino received favourable reviews for their sweaters and négligés, their studios stopped the conveyor belts and concentrated on polishing up these semi-precious gems into two of the most shimmering stars of all time. Julia Turner was made more exotic by MGM – her auburn hair was dyed blonde and her name was changed to Lana – while Margarita Cansino's Latin edges were eroded by Columbia – her black hair was dyed bright red and her name was changed to her mother's unmarried name of Rita Hayworth – presumably so that the boys abroad could have their bit of spice while remaining unconfused about their Anglo-Saxon loyalties. Turner and Hayworth were manufactured, but they were also magical.

Lana Turner was a serious sex dream, sometimes a little too solid to be a vamp, but she walked that path and sometimes turned in shockingly sympathetic performances, such as in *Ziegfield Girl* when she steals the film from the formidable competition of Judy Garland and Hedy Lamarr, as she fights to keep hold of her sugar daddy-donated apartment, *and* her pride in the eyes of her parents. When Turner and John Garfield go into the big clinch on the beach during *The Postman Always Rings Twice* they are *primitive* cave people despite her platinum hair – they are just such dumb, gorgeous hunks, and so snowblind, so mad for each other, that murdering her husband is the only thing within the realms of their capability. Turner was married seven times, and seemed to become a better and yet number actress with each disastrous end. Her confused, corrupted face played into the hands of the narcissistic, bound-for-oblivion women she was to play in the Fifties, the ageing actress of *Imitation Of Life* and the absinthe addict of *Madame X*.

Even bigger and better than Turner was Rita Hayworth. One thinks of Hayworth painted and coiffed to perfection, lounging on a king-size or a real king's bed – overdressed if wearing more than a négligé. Yet dancing, her first skill and possibly the only skill she ever believed she possessed, was what made her look happy, especially when she got the chance to dance with Fred Astaire in *You Were Never Lovelier*. She was a sweet and non-malicious beauty – Shelley Winters recalls with warm shock the way Hayworth, the studio's star, took the fat young contract player to her heart and found strategic parts for her to play in Hayworth vehicles. She seemed to grow more tender with time and with each new divorce, rather than tougher à la Turner. The difference in their personalities can be seen in the way they live now: Miss Turner facelifted, making guest appearances in TV soap operas, stubbornly preserving herself, and Miss Hayworth a recluse, and declared senile at a shockingly young age. Marilyn Monroe is

Lana Turner: from Schwab's to slobs

Lauren Bacall and Bogart in *To Have And Have Not*

seen by many as *the* Hollywood tragedy, but the title is Miss Hayworth's. Marilyn was always Marilyn; she used up every bit of Marilyn-ness she had. But Rita Hayworth, like her second husband Orson Welles, is one of the great wasted resources of our time – good, brilliant, but not quite resilient.

Turner and Hayworth were the 'Being' Vamps; so were Ann Sheridan, Jean Wallace, Gloria Grahame, Evelyn Keyes, Paulette Goddard, Gene Tierney and Jennifer Jones. As the War wore on and the Allies had all but won, a newer, tougher kind of girl became popular – the 'Doing' Vamp. She was best portrayed by the nineteen-year-old Lauren Bacall in *To Have And Have Not*, but Claire Trevor, Lizbeth 'The Threat' Scott, Alexis Smith, Susan Hayward, Ida Lupino, Ella Raines, Barbara Stanwyck and Audrey Totter also had a shot at her. Even Tallulah Bankhead, who had been vamping around from stage to screen to society columns for two decades, found some measure of success as a vamp of the Doing variety in Alfred Hitchcock's *Lifeboat*.

Why was she wanted? Maybe men had spent so many years in each other's company and enjoyed it that they were ready for a woman who was a little more like a man. Maybe they needed no more morale boosters in tight sweaters because their morale could get no higher. Still, there she was: not really a career girl – catch *any* vamp working late at the office or fumbling for the alarm clock – but not one to sit on a silk cushion and pose for posterity. Bacall and her brigade turned up on boats or in speakeasies or in trouble as singers, thieves, strangers, wearing tailored suits, smouldering seriously above starched collars. All day she waited for the night; everything in her past had been for the best and tomorrow was waiting, grooming itself for her as she was for it. She shared a common code of decency and thrills with Bogart or Mitchum or Gable and she loved nothing more than to engage him in verbal Indian wrestling across a crowded table. She wore her brain on her sleeve and she was not for the weak.

Vamp's last gasp combined the glamour of the Being with the guts of the Doing in the person of a sharecropper's daughter from North Carolina. Her name was Lucy Johnson and her alias was Ava Gardner, but there was little difference between the two. The girl was a gypsy; she had wandered like a gypsy through marriages to Mickey Rooney and Artie Shaw, into films, she dismissed a panting Howard Hughes as her 'personal pilot', cared not a damn that she was being groomed as *the* MGM idol to succeed Lana Turner – she boasted that she had been to business school and would make a damn good secretary – and treated the smitten crooning king Frank Sinatra as a mere admirer (even when they were married), interchangeable with the bullfighters she collected like poker chips. She was the flip, already hip, side of the simpering, hysterical Southern Belle – dark, dangerous and devastating. White trash was never more lovely to look at.

Ava Gardner: the barefaced Contessa

She even treated the movies in this cavalier fashion – go to Hollywood, make a few films, get some money, go to Spain; go back to Hollywood, make a few films, get some money, go to London. Hollywood had never been used like this before yet there were no available starlets whose beauty was up to Gardner's. They let themselves be used until her beauty ran out, they let her play gypsy on and off the screen, but Hollywood never again created a vamp.

Think about the Fifties. Sputnik – Elvis – Korea – Marilyn! All these things were causes or effects of that morning in the Fifties when the American Dream woke up, decided that it didn't feel itself and slowly mutated into the American Disease. Grown rich from the fat of the War, it should have been a decade of celebration for America, yet it was a decade of self-recrimination. It should have been time for a party, instead it was time for paranoia. The foreign Reds had the Bomb and no regard for the 38th Parallel while the domestic Reds were under every Mom's bed and running Hollywood, according to Senator Joe McCarthy. Teenage, that long hot howl of discontent, was starting, on the streets in the shape of the first gang rumbles and on the screen choreographed by the Russian Konstantin Stanislavsky via the Strasberg's Actors Studio in the shape of the Method. Tin Pan Alley's Moon in June pap was being swamped by white boys who wanted to be black, in their vanguard a Momma's boy from Tupelo, Mississippi. Speaking of which, the Negroes wanted their part of the late

Dream and were marching for it in the South. It was a time of widespread fear, a time for the loss of innocence and the perpetuation of ignorance. It was a decade of panic. America wanted answers and it wanted them fast. If you could locate, diagnose and offer a cure for the American Disease then you were in business. It was in the Fifties that America got on the couch and it has never really stood up since. If the answers were spurious and stunk of superstition it hardly mattered.

Hence the rise of Senator McCarthy and the House Un-American Activities Committee.

Hence the rise of fatuous pop psychology.

Come the hour, come the expert.

The seeds of American male malcontent had been smouldering for a long time. During the Second World War psychological screening methods were used by the draft boards for the first time and over two million men were rejected for lacking the ability to 'face life, live with others, think for themselves and stand on their own two feet.' Hot on the heels of this, the none too successful novelist Philip Wylie wrote *Generation Of Vipers* in which he invented the theory of 'Momism' to explain the ineffectiveness of the American male: 'Mom is everywhere and everything and damned near everybody, and from her depends all the rest of the US. Disguised as good old mom, dear old mom, sweet old mom, your loving mom and so on, she is the bride at every funeral and the corpse at every wedding.'

Instead of dismissing the man as a raving hysteric, psychologists immediately embraced Momism as a *fact*. Of course! It was soon discovered what all criminals, inadequates and misfits had in common – they all had a MOTHER! Every last one of them!

When Mom wasn't crushing the American male at home, the Commies were crushing him abroad. The Korean War was the first real chance America had had to fight face to face with Communism, and America failed dismally. Seven thousand American soldiers were captured by North Koreans; a massive one-seventh succumbed to brainwashing. They went home to America declaring that the War had been a result of US imperialism and aggression. America was horrified by its own weakness and by the strength of the Communists, strength that it first watched in action during the Second World War when the Russians never dealt with less than two-thirds of the German Army. The comforting insults that were and still are flung at liberals at home – egghead, sex pervert, drug addict, weak freak – could not be flung at the foreign Communists any more.

On 7 October 1957, the final straw happened in the shape of Sputnik, the world's first orbital satellite, and the start of the space race. It was a body blow to the American ego, such as it was – the richest nation on the face of the earth, yet the heavens were the sovereign territory of a bunch of god-damned *atheists*!

The first childcare experts went to the Soviet Union and came back stunned that the children were 'warm, spontaneous, polite and generous.' Spock, who had advocated permissiveness in the bringing up of children, changed his tune. He announced that the Russians were inspired by their sense of common purpose and love of their country, which American youth conspicuously lacked. A bestseller of 1955, *Why Johnny Can't Read* was followed by the ominous *Why Ivan Can Read*.

The answers America was getting about its poor performance were sounding more and more as though it was *America's* fault. So they stopped looking for answers and turned to rewritten history and reassurance, big and smothering on the screen, to help them forget. No one reassured America better than John Wayne, and he rose from being a B-actor of the Thirties and Forties to the dizzy heights of winning all wars four times a year in the Fifties. In real life he had never fought in any war – but who wanted real life? It was too frightening. The western returned in all its tatty glory and Americans watched Indians being massacred to their hearts' content. Okay, so it had been a genocidal war, but it was a war they *won*, that's the point.

Elsewhere on the screen, Dean Martin and Jerry Lewis tried to laugh your troubles away and the popular *Invasion* films revealed that the reason why Americans were not acting like the legendary pioneers was because the real Americans had been stolen away by creatures from Outer Space and replaced by cold, calculating automatons. These creatures were obviously crypto-Russians, not so much Little Green as Little Red Men.

Young people used the cinema as a mirror too, preferring to see their bad times reflected, rather than their good times. The Fifties was the decade of the 'masculine brute rebellion' and the Angry Young Men, except it was not so much *anger* as the belly-aching of brats in a playpen. Post-War young men, from Marlon Brando to John Braine, whined about everything from the state of the world to the way their girlfriend had ironed their shirts. In retrospect they are ridiculous but at the time they were taken ridiculously seriously as a symptom of America's malaise. The most angry thing about these young actors was that there were a lot of them who'd come onto the market after studying drama on the GI Bill and they were damn well going to make sure that all the juicy movie roles didn't keep going to *women*. Moms and actresses! They'll all barbecue a poor boy's balls given half a chance!

Angry was the last thing women were allowed to be in the Fifties. To make sure the crumbling man *felt* like a man, women had to retreat from the gains they had made. There could be no more strong women like Crawford or even frightening beauties like Hayworth. Both kinds of women were too mature. To make men feel big, women had to be little girls, looking up. They had to be Sex Dolls.

The whole Sex Doll syndrome was so horrible that it would have com-busted after a few films had it not had the chance to wrap itself around the glowing persona of Marilyn Monroe. Like John Wayne, she had been shunted from pillar to post, from studio to studio in the Feisty Forties. But now her country needed her and she did her duty like a good Sex Doll. She became capitalism's curvaceous carrot, dangled under the nose of the Corporation Man. The Corporation Man, as if you needed to be told, was – yes! – yet another pop psychologist's attempt to get a finger on the pulse of the American Disease. He was the harassed hero of the 1950 bestseller *The Lonely Crowd* and he sang the swan-song of capitalism – no ideals to aspire to, no wild country to tame. It was belly-aching at its best – the man who had everything and wanted none of it! Shekels as shackles! Affluence as castration! No longer a pioneer but a pawn on the boss man's chessboard! It was hard for the American male, living that soft. All he wanted was to trade in his Corvette for a cowboy's pony...until he met Marilyn.

Marilyn is always talking about millionaires – diamonds, stocks and bonds are what she wants, not sex. What she admires in a man is not looks, guts or glory but MONEY. She is the opulent opiate, the voluptuous Valium of the Corporation Man, who has nothing but his salary to recommend him. Monroe comes across as an idiot in most of her films simply because the men she is chasing are physical and emotional dwarfs, the sort of men that self-respecting girls simply do not chase. When she finally faces a sex-ually appetizing man, such as Tony Curtis or Jack Lemmon, he must be made ridiculous by being dressed up as a woman so as not to make the Corporation Man feel rejected. To make capitalism even more precious to the Corporation Man, more *his*, it was a mystery to which the Sex Doll had no access. Harlow and Crawford might consciously use their market assets to move up the social scale or get a better flat, but the Sex Doll was dependent on the Corporation Man's mercy. The Sugar Daddy had always existed, but the balance of power had never been tilted so ridiculously to-wards him before. Lana Turner's in *Ziegfield Girl* is tall, dark and handsome and not even old enough to be her father; Marilyn's are short, bald and talk boring waffle in silly high voices. No matter! They have *money*. If you work hard for your corporation you too will get money – and a girl who's a pale imitation of this. Let's face it, she *has* to love you for your money – she could certainly never love you for anything else.

As Marilyn helps the Corporation Man to learn to love capitalism, she quells his fear of flaming youth, youth wild in a way that the Corporation Man probably never was and now never will be with a hausfrau and a Mom and a double garage and a bottomless frigidaire to support. Although Mar-ilyn is young and beautiful, there is never any chance that she will play opposite Brando or Dean or Clift as the atypical Fifties brunette beauties do

– Elizabeth Taylor and Natalie Wood, whose striking mature brands of beauty are allowed to run riot because both girls made it as juveniles and now cannot be done away with to make the world safe for Sex Dolls – because if the Placebo and the Problem meet and fight, then of course the Placebo will lay down and die. Every time Marilyn melts for a barrel-bellied menopausal millionaire she tells the Corporation Man, 'Gee, I don't care about the muscles rippling out of that Brando guy's torn T-shirt...I don't care about James Dean's swimming-pool eyes...don't care for Clift's bruised beauty...*you've* got what I want. *Now* can I open that charge account at Tiffany's?'

At the start of her film career, Marilyn was allowed to play sexy broads with psychological problems – *Don't Bother To Knock*'s babysitter, Rose Loomis in *Niagara* – but as the Fifties wore on and the problems got worse, she was needed more and more as a muscle relaxant and underwent a celluloid lobotomy, leaving her free to play women with no brain at all quite happily. Her libido left too; no more Rose Loomis yearning after anonymous young toughs and kissing under waterfalls, sending up steam from Niagara! She became the complete Sex Doll, magnificently fashioned and totally unable to feel anything, anywhere.

Here they are now behind her, the legions of Sex Dolls, millions of them advancing like clockwork toys, waiting for her to fall over or OD or die. They are Mamie Van Doren, Terry Moore, Sheree North, Connie Stevens, Sandra Giles, Zsa Zsa Gabor, Anita Ekberg. They are nearly always blonde; before the Fifties there was no Blonde Fever, the Love Goddesses had gone all across the spectrum from dark blondes like Dietrich to redheads like Hayworth to brunettes like Gardner. Blondes were so unheralded that both Harlow and Turner took advantage of black and white film to play explosive redheads; in the opening moments of the late Thirties' *Ninotchka*, the narrative talks of the good old days when 'sirens were brunettes, not things on police cars.' But for the crumbling man, blonde is essential – blonde, like a little girl! Shirley Temple with sex appendages! But even when she is not blonde, a Sex Doll is still a boring Sex Doll: Jane Russell, launched by Howard Hughes in 1943, only made two more films in the Forties – in the Fifties she never stopped working, becoming Doyenne of Deep Breaths and Dull Acting. Even from the country of Celia Johnson and Kay Kendall came a school for Sex Dolls. The overseer was J. Arthur Rank, and the girls were Susan Shaw, Sandra Dorne, Diana Dors, Belinda Lee and Joan Rice. For once Britons were as dumb as Americans – all Sex Dolls are created equal. Even the nice girls of the Thirties and Forties talk disparagingly of men when men deserve it – Claudette Colbert in *Boomtown* says she left her home town because of the measly men, 'Men you wouldn't shake a stick at!' – but the Sex Doll looks at anything in trousers and says 'Gee'... and she's a red carpet at his feet.

Zsa Zsa Gabor: the most notorious Hungarian since Chopin, not averse to chopin' around herself

Diana Dors: Mother Courage as Baby Doll

Jeanne Crain: V, but not for victory

Debbie Reynolds: the power of positive thinking, before Hurricane Liz

For occasional contrast, there was the Nice Doll – Debbie Reynolds leaping about mindlessly, Doris Day dithering – or the Sex Boy – Audrey Hepburn tagging along looking up at you like a wide-eyed, sweet-smelling little brother – but one thing there was no room for in the Fifties was girls with skills. Skills are not needed in a world where women are only ever spectators – no more Ginger Rogers or Esther Williams or Eleanor Powell or Sonja Henie or Ann Miller. Not even humour is allowed any more: whereas we laughed *with* Jean Harlow, we laugh *at* her Fifties heiress, Judy Holliday.

An even more sickening sight than the Sex Dolls on parade is the roll-call of careers that were invalidated by the vogue. Jeanne Crain, the sensitive and sensual Forties film star, tried to become a pin-up even though she had seven children! Anne Baxter, the scheming minx of *All About Eve*, tried the same thing and met the same fate. Lola Albright was cast in straight Sex Doll parts when she was obviously the American Dietrich. The American Garbo, Faye Emerson, gave up in disgust and married into high society. Anne Bancroft, so popular in the Sixties as Mrs Robinson, actually started her film career in 1952 and made no waves until middle age. Susan Cabot, the beautiful singer, was pushed into Sex-Doll-at-home roles. Lauren Bacall, at her lynx-like peak at nineteen in 1944, was pushed into older confidante roles before she was thirty. Linda Darnell, *Forever Amber* of 1947, was matronly in the Fifties, as was Joanne Dru. Anne Francis was promoted by MGM in 1952's *Lydia Bailey* as a Turneresque sexpot when sophisticated comedy was her forte. The lovely and sultry Swedes Marta Toren and Signe Hasso, brought to Hollywood at the end of the Forties, went home at the start of the Fifties. The spectacular Julie London, who would have made a glorious vamp, gave up films in the mid-Fifties to go into the aural equivalent of vamping – torch singing.

Established stars did no better – rather they did worse; they were savaged instead of subdued for all the juicy parts they had pulverized in the Thirties and Forties. To be fair to the Fifties, they had never pretended that they were going to be merciful to prima donnas. The decade started with two films that had the hatchet out for women in general and actresses in particular, *All About Eve* and *Sunset Boulevard*, in which women recited man-made lines to comfort men – that fame was a sham, that all they wanted was a man. Still, one line rings true. 'You were a big star once,' says William Holden to Gloria Swanson. 'I'm still big. It's the pictures that got small.'

Too small for Crawford: the Joan Crawford of the Thirties and Forties had been considered a beauty more than worthy of Clark Gable; overnight in the Fifties she was pleading with unknown wimps like Cliff Robertson for their affection. *Then* she had played ambitious beauties, and the two descriptions had gone together easily; *now* the word *ambitious* translated

Called to the bar: Sinatra and Hayworth, stranded in the Fifties, clink highballs and high hopes in *Pal Joey*

into Mom-ridden American as *battleaxe*, and Crawford's bow-tie mouth and glittery, glass-like eyes, copied as the peak of chic by *Vogue* cover girls in the Forties, were recoiled from as grotesque.

Susan Hayward, who played gorgeous gutsy broads in the Forties, now found herself playing Tartar princesses to John Wayne's Genghis Khan (typecasting!). Even Rita Hayworth was given rubbish, though her beauty was still intact, until in 1957 she was cast with Frank Sinatra and Columbia's premier Sex Doll Kim Novak in *Pal Joey*. Sinatra looks poleaxed by Hayworth whenever he is near her – so does the simple Polack, Miss Novak.

Some went running. Piper Laurie was the female Tony Curtis, so beautiful in Technicolor and baubles that a decal was all she was ever allowed to be. She and Curtis pranced through an endless Casbah till the mid-Fifties, and it took its toll on both of them. Curtis would later try to write novels, get treated like a piece of dumb ass and go into a sanatorium to recover from a nervous breakdown. More pragmatically, Piper Laurie gave up Hollywood and went to learn the skill of stage acting before returning to films in Sixties deglamorized roles and notching up two Oscar nominations, most notably for *The Hustler*.

The Sex Doll worked well into the Sixties – mostly in the pouting person of bovine blondies like Novak and Elke Sommer (how far from that other German blonde, Miss Dietrich). Girls like these either looked very stupid or

Mansfield: manslaughter or just GBH? Jayne and friend interrupted while discussing Schlegel

very thoughtful on screen; probably they were both. She fell from her pedestal – up there, crucified on some locker room wall – when Norma Jean had been and gone and America awoke one morning to find that its best Sex Doll was Jayne Mansfield, as ugly as Marilyn was beautiful with a head full of straw and lips like something at the bottom of a pond – the ultimate numb blonde. She was the pâté de foie gras of Sex – stuffed to ugly bursting point. The girl couldn't help it – but she had to go.

She was done away with unceremoniously – more of a mercy killing than anything else. The vamp was hunted down like the fox she was, run to earth and tossed to the mob in the mezzanine. But a cub got away and came back across the Atlantic in a film canister as the English Girl, the Girl From Nowhere, the *Darling*.

When Julie Christie won the Oscar in 1965 for alluring, enticing and vampiring helpless men, Jayne Mansfield had taken off her make-up and was making an ass of herself in her sole bid for credibility, *Single Room Furnished*. It was so dire that it did not merit showing until her death in 1967. No fool like a Sex Doll – *that* wasn't the way to do it. Although the vamp was never American again, she was too good to be forgotten. Jayne Mansfield dreamed of playing Harlow till the day she died. 'Who *is* that chick?' said the American pop star Joan Jett when she saw a picture of Marilyn Monroe on my wall. The vamp – loser and still champ!

Chapter Three
BEAUTY AND CORRUPTION

The rich are different – they have scandal. Scandal demands money. Without it, scandal would be at worst crime and at best sordid. But the word scandal conjures up juicy sideshows spontaneously staged for the work-dimmed eyes of clock-watchers and card-punchers who gain malicious and righteous pleasure from seeing their betters and richers and keepers undone.

Whereas crime ends in punishment and sordid episodes are quickly forgotten, scandal slips out of the cell, scattering banknotes and blank cheques à la Appleseed and lives on for ever, handed down like prole folklore.

Hollywood is the family seat of American scandal. In the early half of the twentieth century the name occupied the unhallowed ground of the Middle American psyche in the way that New York City does today: where people run to to become dope fiends and floosies, where foreigners prey, where crime pays. Indeed, it was alien in a way that the East Coast could never be – inherited from the Indians, the Spanish and the Mexicans, full of Hispanic siren-sounding towns, the heat, the earthquakes, the desert, the various things growing on trees, and all you have to do is reach up and pick them...sanctuary of sin!

Sanctuary of scandal. Scandal demands money and there has always been money in California, though Wall Street is on the other side of the land. Wall Street is starched collars and serious business – no swimming-pools or Happy Hours. The money on Wall Street is sensible stocks and bonds but the wealth of California is pure pagan gold, two thousand million dollars worth tugged out of the ground by ten thousand men all working separately, desperately, refusing to band together and co-operate. Savage sanctuary: justice meant lynching because there was no time to build prisons, no time to build anything until the last precious drop of yellow was squeezed out of the earth like priceless pus.

There were lots of millionaires in early Hollywood – the smaller ones were the studio heads, the swarthy boys off the boat who told a story and found glory. The big ones were men who made their money elsewhere – mostly from their father's Last Will and Testament – and took it to Hollywood to have fun and influence starlets. Cabots and Lowells, Mellons and Paleys might stay in the chic shade of the East – Hollywood is a town of arrivistes, and the millionaires who arrived had as little time for good taste as the gaudiest B-girl.

The Twenties drew to Hollywood thousands of girls who wanted to be in the pictures as well as early specimens of the genus hustler who smelt easy money and journalists who smelt sensation. Advertisements for 'Schools of Photoplay Acting' were everywhere. BE A MOVIE ACTOR OR ACTRESS! LET MILLIONS LEARN TO APPLAUD YOUR APPEARANCES ON THE SCREEN! BE LOVED AND LAUDED BY THE MIGHTY PUBLIC! BE KNOWN IN THE PALACES OF THE GREAT AND WEALTHY AND IN THE COTTAGES OF THE LOWLY! proclaimed the ads. Soon all the waitress jobs were taken and girls drifted into prostitution. To avoid the California vagrancy laws they invariably gave their occupation as 'movie extra'. Boarding houses showed signs saying ROOMS FOR RENT – NO DOGS OR ACTORS ALLOWED. There were constant headlines like THREE BEAUTIFUL FILM STARS ARRESTED IN BAWDY HOUSE. Stories of sex, drugs and drunkenness crept into the national papers. A series of specific incidents established Hollywood as a hothouse of hysterical hedonism. There was the never-solved murder of the director William Desmond Taylor, which revealed his associations with two reigning favourites of the silent screen, Mary Miles Minter and Mabel Normand. Miles Minter's hot letters to the director blotted her lily-white copybook. Normand was cleared of any association with his death, but shortly afterwards at a drinking party at the home of Chaplin leading lady Edna Purviance, Normand's chauffeur shot another male guest.

Virginia Rappe, young star of two-reel comedies, attended the near-constant drinking party held by Roscoe 'Fatty' Arbuckle, ex-plumber and obese buffoon, at the St Francis Hotel. After an interlude behind locked doors, Rappe died from 'chronic pelvic illness'. The inside story has it that Arbuckle, in a drunken and impotent rage, raped Rappe with a broken bottle, though he was acquitted by three juries of any responsibility. The prejudice of the juries is clear and callous – any girl who went to Hollywood deserved what she got, even a broken bottle.

The Taylor murder was said to have sold more papers than any other incident in US history. Arbuckle, Miles Minter and Normand were all forcibly retired and their films, representing an investment of millions, were withdrawn. The nation was still chewing over these cautionary tales when the clean-cut actor Wallace Reid died at the age of thirty, and was revealed to have been a heroin addict.

The nation was stunned and this time the studios were scared too. They felt guilty and foreign. The competition between them had been so fierce that they had not stopped to worry about American moral standards – the only American morals they knew were Hollywood morals, which meant no morals. Selznick, Fox, Zukor, Goldwyn, Loew, Laemmle and the rest grouped together to perform a magnificent penance – not only would they clean up Hollywood but they would let an outsider wield the broom and have the final say on what was good and what was not.

The dustpan and brush were picked up by a man steeped in deep American decency – Will Hays, Postmaster General and Presbyterian elder. The first thing he did was invent the morals clause in the contract which meant the player could be cancelled if found guilty of having a good time. Then he drew up the Production Code to limit onscreen depravity. It was a brilliant Public Relations exercise on the part of the studios but little else – you could show whatever you wanted on the screen, so long as the wrong-doers were punished (a recipe that DeMille – who now of course supported the Hays Office all the way – had perfected in his Sex, Sadism and Sodom epics years before). Morals clauses were a good way of getting rid of un-wanted players, but big stars like Clara Bow were still allowed to have their way – have their way with a whole football team, in Clara's case. America

If I only had a brain: not the Tin Man, certainly not the Thin Man, but Fatty Arbuckle

would never really clean up Hollywood in the real sense of placing limits on the rich and protection on the poor — that's not good capitalism, and California was making the American government very rich very fast. Just like after the Gold Rush when the Union, blinded by the stuff that was growing in the ground, made California a State without asking it to go through the usual motions of being a Territory — for money it had made an exception of California once and for money it would do so again.

So California ruled itself as a fiefdom, free of normal moral constraints, and the tragic lives of Hollywood's saddest and sweetest stars — the suicides and addictions and constant sorrows that plagued them right into the Fifties — can be seen being sown in the earliest years of the film capital, when a handful of robber barons ruled the rough land around the Hollywood sign — give *me* your weak and I'll eat them up! Serfs toiled on casting couches and the unholy trinity of Hollywood — MONEY, SEX, DEATH — was formulated and refined and established like a secret coat-of-arms.

Money. America has two kinds of that stinking by-product of capitalism, the gangster — most of them are criminals and a few are millionaires. To understand America you must comprehend its millionaires, particularly the millionaires who settled on Hollywood like flies on a Danish pastry. In the days of the New Deal and the War effort there was Texan Howard Hughes who liked to fly alone and fall in love like a schoolboy in sneakers with film stars as diverse as Katharine Hepburn and Ava Gardner while grooming units of pure gorgeousness like Harlow and Lollo. He went loopy as the American Dream became the Disease, refusing to cut his hair and toenails while insisting that germs and Communists were launching a two-pronged attack on him — to give him a cold and steal his silver while he was incapacitated, no doubt. A comical American tragedy.

In the trashy and savage days of Appeasement and the Depression there was Joe Kennedy, American — and there was William Randolph Hearst, Citizen. George Hearst dug gold out of the ground — he was one of the Forty-Niners and as such could afford to be illiterate while he mounted up more millions than he could count. He bought a seat in the Senate and a newspaper. His son, William Randolph, was barely in long trousers before he seized the paper and conned eight million dollars out of his mother. Then, with a crassness amazing even for turn-of-the-century America, he brought journalism down to the gutter and gave bloody birth to the tabloid as it is today — all hysteria and hypocrisy, parading dirt while decrying it while insisting on the public's right to know.

Hearst was a crazed patriot, the political kiss of death to any cause. He met the up-and-coming German statesman A. Hitler and advised him on the way to make friends with and influence Americans. He went into films with the sole aim of buying his simpering little girlfriend Marion Davies into stardom; Hearst's bedtime bent can be detected through Miss Davies'

Gina Lollobrigida looking like a continent waiting to be discovered repeated roles as girls who pretended to be boys and were disrobed in the last reel. The public never took to her and when the great Mae West made a crack about Davies' acting ability, the adulterous Hearst went to town and in 1936 ran an editorial attacking her. 'Isn't it about time the United States did something about Mae West?' it seethed before going on to call her 'a monster of lubricity' and 'a menace to the sacred institution of the American family.'

Hearst's real genius was his Lifestyle – he was the first practitioner of the now hackneyed Trash Aesthetic. It was to describe Hearst that the phrase 'the last of the big spenders' was coined, and the spending was principally done on the Hearst Castle, San Simeon. In a display of disgusting taste never since equalled, San Simeon was created between the Pacific and the Santa Lucia mountains. In it was all the worst of America's attitude to Europe; Hearst went at Europe and its civilization like a hog at the trough. Ivory towers overlooked a 240,000 acre ranch that stretched for fifty miles. Still unfinished at Hearst's death in 1951, this cross between a Spanish cathedral, Roman palace and Gothic castle contained thirty-eight bedrooms, thirty-one bathrooms and a cinema. Guests were housed in three adjacent castlettes consisting of another forty-six rooms. Orson Welles in *Citizen Kane* shot it as a nightmare rather than a dream home, full of shadows and stagnancy and loneliness; he knew it better than the men who laid the foundations and built up the bricks.

In the grounds monkeys, cheetahs, lions, leopards and panthers were caged as thirteenth-century Madonna and Childs, Roman mosaic floors and fifteenth-century Flemish tapestries were caged inside. His henchmen pillaged the world again and again, and even though the house was so large there was not room for one quarter of the treasures he took, so they lay dead to the world in unopened crates in the Hearst cellars.

While half of California struggled to live through the Depression, Hearst partied on his father's money. The intelligent poor hated him. The stupid poor envied him. Anyhow the name stank. His son Randolph spent his life living down the Hearst name, channelling much of the wealth into charitable foundations and turning San Simeon over to the State as a tourist attraction. He hid in adopted Catholicism and had children. One of these children, Patricia, would later be captured in the Seventies by a band of confused would-be revolutionaries who were sure of just one thing – they hated America and wanted it to crawl. What better way than to twist a Hearst's wrist? The first of the gang's demands was the feeding of twenty thousand Los Angeles poor – very illegal, but what a change from the law-abiding greed of Citizen Hearst during the Depression! Patricia thought so too and joined this band of many colours; middle-class white girls, working-class Hispanic and Oriental girls and black men. She sent virulent tape-recordings to her family, whom she now addressed as 'the pig Hearst'.

The sins of the grandfather...

Like a good heiress, she somehow survived the police ambush that consumed the other members of the gang. The rich get reformed and the rest get – machine-gunned! A Hearst is a Hearst is the *worst*.

The Kennedys, on the other hand, moved from paupers to princes in one generation. Joe Kennedy, son of a saloon-keeper, grew rich from acting as capitalism's pimp; he acted as overseer to stock-pools on Wall Street, buying shares to make lame ducks look like winners, encouraging the hard-pressed public with dreams of free money to rush to buy the shares as the prices soared and Joe's stock-pool sold, reaping vast profits and leaving egg on Joe Public's *Wall Street Journal*.

Not surprisingly, he was never respected back East. When a Boston newspaper (although Boston is today considered an Irish city and although the later Kennedys are painted as society swells, Boston has always been the seat of Eastern Protestant aristocracy and the only participants these people will recognize are those of English Puritan descent) called him 'an Irishman', he bellowed, 'I was born here! My parents were born here! What do I have to do to get called an American?'

Go West, old man.

Before the Wall Street Crash of 1929, Kennedy had turned his sights towards the Hollywood sign – another chance to get rich, another chance to be called an American amongst people who wouldn't ask to see your pedigree. He went to Hollywood to finance – playing a major part in the setting up of RKO, Radio Pictures Corporation – to produce – though he found himself unhappy with the intangibles of creativity – and to pick up non-Catholic, usable girls; one girl in particular, one Josephine Klanowsky turned Gloria Swanson, whom he made what the gossip columns of the day euphemistically called his 'protégée'.

In her teens, Swanson was an angular and tacky Mack Sennet bathing belle; in her prime she was a silent spit-curled coquette whose mannered melodrama and lousy posture stood astride the silent screen like a clumsy colossus. In retrospect, even Gloria in her prime was puny – at the time hash-slingers stood at their mirrors and strained to see her.

The coming of sound exposed her grating Chicago twang and spirited away her popularity. The coming of Joe Kennedy, for all his millions of dollars and strings to be pulled, could not put Gloria together again. Her liaison with Joe Kennedy was the low-point of her career.

She was already in her mid-thirties when she was taken under his wing. Although his protection helped her to find steady work through such unforgettables as *What A Widow!* and *Screen Snapshots No.4*, Joe Kennedy was the harbinger of the leanest days Swanson ever knew, a mediocre spread sandwiched between Cecil B. DeMille's society Salome and *Sunset Boulevard*. Swanson eventually rejected everything Joe Kennedy stood for

Gloria Swanson poses with a mouth even bigger than Joe Kennedy's

by doing Europe and hooking herself the Marquis de la Falaise de Coudray as her third husband – one of those ten a penny wandering French aristos with more manners than money. But that didn't matter – she was a Marquise! She, the hash-slingers' heroine!

As for slow old Joe himself, he learned – like Citizen Hearst – that the public cannot be force-fed a fantasy; what comes over great in the bedroom may not come across so great at the box-office. It took his career as a politician – and his repeated calls for America not to fall out with that nice Herr Hitler – for the world to realize that here was a man who deserved to be called an American.

Sex. Rule One: the sun will rise in the East. Rule Two: wherever there are rich men trying not to feel old there will be young girls trying not to feel poor.

In these post-hedonist, head-searching days of America's life there are probably more young actresses labouring on analysts' couches than on the casting kind. (In the Sixties the top casting directors became women so that the old stories could stick no more – but doesn't the recent spate of dumb and docile TV actors with nothing but their pectorals to recommend them indicate a revival of the Chaise of Shame? Except these days it would be a jacuzzi.) But before Man's favourite sport became jogging – especially in the Twenties' celebration of celluloid's coming of age and the Fifties' frantic wake — Hollywood was a hotbed of hot beds.

The massive (but not moral) majority of the acquisitive action went on on the periphery of stardom. When a studio saw a girl who had something they could sell for sure — a Harlow or a Hayworth — there was no need for her to give it away, as it were — she was simply too valuable to offend. The idea of some greasy little lecher chasing Greta Garbo, for instance, around a king-size business desk is raucously ridiculous. But when a mildly pretty girl who looked like a million others — as opposed to a million dollars — wanted walk-on work there was one sure way of auditioning that would make sure she was remembered — at least until some other girl did it better. Another kind of screen test — these are the screens you pull down to shut out the world.

Millions more secretaries, stenographers and shorthand typists have slept with their bosses than have actresses — there is a story in every High Street — but it can be excused because it didn't *get* them anywhere, and can be rationalized and purified by the secretary's traditional role of status symbol crossed with nursery nurse, a logical extension of her all-round nurturing niche. On the casting couch the deal was cold and clear-eyed and only a loose change jangle away from actual prostitution. The couch could make his little girl a call-girl! — it became the inanimate bogeyman of every American father whose dairy-fresh daughter had run away from Heartland USA dreaming of screenings and sunshine and success. Casting couch sex was seen as the archetypal Hollywood sex, and it was in that it was a game in which the man called the shots, held the power and could welch on the deal: it was an epic magnification of more boring market-places and punier power games.

Many variations of the act were allowed in Hollywood, all but one — the one in which the girl stepped out of line. Then Hollywood was a small town with mangling morals.

The Norwegian and beatific blonde Ingrid Bergman was a hot property in Forties Hollywood — she played selfless Lefty Madonnas in *Casablanca* and *For Whom The Bell Tolls* whose purity of soul was so white-light blinding that their commitment to liberal causes could be completely overlooked. She became one of America's most popular stars — her shorn head in *For Whom The Bell Tolls* became a much-copied hairdo known as the Maria — and she was also a symbol of purity, being not only married but to a DOCTOR! Her morals made haloes look like L-plates, glowed America. It was so happy it had settled down with Ingrid Bergman.

In 1949 Miss Bergman left Hollywood for a short stay in Italy to make a film under the Italian director Roberto Rossellini. *Under* was the operative word because later that year Miss Bergman revealed that she and Rossellini were expecting a happy event — and it *wasn't* an Oscar.

The outcry all across America was hysterical and deafening. Her films were withdrawn from release and she was denounced from the floor of the Senate, where hysterical politicians made it clear that someone who got their kicks filling the water supply with leprosy germs would be more worthy of respect than Ingrid Bergman.

In 1950 the fallen idol had twins – the sin was complete, and doubled! In my view, though, the *real* sin was nothing to do with adulteries or pregnancies or babies – it was the fact that Rossellini lured Ingrid Bergman away from Hollywood and subjected her to nothing but his rotten boring art films for years solid until the new marriage broke up and she returned to a forgetful Hollywood (busy oohing and aahing at the scantily-clad sins of the Sex Dolls) to win her second Academy Award for *Anastasia*.

Another variation on the original Hollywood sin of sleeping with someone who couldn't further your career was the blacklist – the roll-call of hopeful young white actresses who slept with or fell in love with or married a Negro. It was only as late as the Fifties that girls got the gall to do this – but even then it was unacceptable to the Hollywood hierarchy. Then men at the top were mostly Jews married to Gentile women, but the hypocrisy of their position was no hindrance to them. It was a white world then and dark pigmentation was thought to be almost a perversion in itself – how doubly perverse, then, is a girl who chooses one of these people in preference to a good white American! A Jew can pass for normal – Harry Cohn even went as far as converting to Catholicism, but a nose job and a name change can change nothing for a Negro.

'Trailblazer' is hardly a word that one thinks of in connection with Kim Novak – to be fair, the simple Chicago-Polish kid was somewhat dwarfed by her times (best Columbia sex symbol succeeding Rita Hayworth; second best Fifties blonde competing with Marilyn Monroe) but nevertheless she rarely gave any celluloid sign that anything was beating inside that décolletage or happening between those earrings. The most spectacular thing she ever did was to fall in love with Sammy Davis Jr, practically Hollywood's only black entertainer, when the whole wholesome white town was lying at her feet.

The news was broken to Harry Cohn (Head of Columbia as well as being the shrewdest Philistine ever to rule a lot with a rod of pig-iron) at a banquet given by a Columbia executive in honour of his brother. Cohn went home after the bash and swallowed bushels of nitroglycerin tablets for his heart condition. His doctor examined him and insisted that he go into hospital. Cohn refused and was treated at home, an electrocardiogram being administered by a heart specialist.

For the first time the Christmas party was not held in Cohn's office. At the studio he wandered about in a daze. The thought of ivory-skinned Kim Novak and positively tar-coloured Sammy Davis Jr getting up to God knows what obsessed him. He finally solved the problem; a call was placed to his 'friends' in Chicago and their lawyer was sent to see him. The lawyer was then sent by Cohn to Davis. No threats of physical violence were believed to have been uttered but the two simple options were made clear – forget Kim Novak or find himself denied employment by any major nightclub in the United States. This couldn't be done? Remember, we're talking America, we're talking gangsters who are pillars of the Establishment. On 10 January 1957, Sammy Davis Jr was married to Loray White, a black Las Vegas dancer.

Soon to follow in Kim Novak's victimized footsteps was Inger Stevens, a smooth, smouldering and enigmatic blonde actress who from 1957 rose towards the big roles until it was discovered in 1960 that she had married a black man. She made only eight films in the next decade – all rot and forgotten – and in 1970, unable to face another decade of nothingness and nastiness, committed suicide with sleeping pills.

Then there was Jean Seberg – a *lucky* girl, picked from thousands by unpleasant Otto Preminger to play *Saint Joan*. She married the French writer Roman Gary (he shot himself in 1980) and spent the Sixties playing a range of roles so eclectic they looked as though they had been picked from a Lucky Dip – lesbians, playgirls, Clint Eastwood's love interest. But at least she worked. In 1970 her marriage cracked; there was involvement with a prominent Black Panther and a miscarriage. The Hollywood scandal rags

Jean Seberg in *Saint Joan*: but no armour was thick enough

Kim Novak: white mischief

Sidney Poitier: black was never more beautiful

gloated over the rumour that the baby would have been *black*. Jean Seberg went to live in Paris, where her career atrophied to the point of not working at all in the three years before she died in 1979 – from an overdose of sleeping pills, slumped in a car a million miles away from the Heartland USA where she was born. Lucky girl...

Sick girls! To chase the kind of man that Lillian Gish had cowered from and Griffith's gang, the good old Klan, had run out of town! It was all a bit too kinky for the film fan to swallow along with their popcorn. Tortured love between white men and black girls (white girls – Ava Gardner, Jennifer Jones – in suntan make-up) had been seen on the screen since the Forties, but it was a tradition made tragic tale – the old plantation patriarch pattern. White girls and black men was altogether too new-fangled and nightmarish for a nation raised on Civil War slop – the slave, literally *on top* at last. It was only with the advent of Sidney Poitier, a man simply too handsome to play anything but sex interest, that black men were thought civilized enough to be in the same room as white girls. After this breakthrough, desperate, dying Hollywood pulled out all the stops for shock appeal and gave us the Shafts, with their black girls downtown and white women uptown, and the Mandingos, black actors and white actresses with no respect for themselves or history pretending that life down on the plantation had been just one long orgy rather than the caged carnage it was. Seberg, Stevens and Novak should have waited a few years and they could have cleaned up – pretending to fuck black men for money instead of loving them for real. Control yourself, corral your emotions and cuddle up to your career when the bed gets too big...

Such was the double-think that slandered multiracial romance while turning divorce into a spectator sport and popularizing it as common currency. One in two Californian marriages break up today as opposed to the modest score of one in three in the other States – how and why did Hollywood start treating marriage like a motel room?

Divorce was always going to be as integral a part of the town as cosmetic surgeons becoming millionaires and the mating call of the casting couch. For the first time there was a State which acted as a magnet for millions of good-looking human beings. Hot and cold physical attraction was everywhere and Mexico – the Nescafé of divorce, where a marriage could end simply by waving a fistful of dollars and a magic wand – was just across the border.

Hollywood razed monogamy, made it a museum piece with the allowance of a level of promiscuity that back home would have got an alley-cat stoned to death outside the city walls. But the easy and sleazy sex could not completely obliterate the sentimental heart of Our Town – Hollywood guys and dolls might use sex like a cup of cocoa but they still carried the shop-soiled dream their parents had practised in High School – the quest for the One.

Unlike Mom and Dad, however, they could afford to make mistakes. Divorce was easily done and there were, as yet, no painful side effects – big fat alimony payments were still a wild, dreaming twinkle in some sharp law student's eye.

Hollywood did not destroy marriage – nowhere was crazier about the sound of wedding bells – but what it did was reduce the wedding ring to the level of a fraternity pin. It made sure that divorce and marriage went together like a horse and carriage. It turned marriage into yet another All-American consumer product.

Hollywood itself did not realize just how acceptable it had made divorce in the eyes of Middle America – Orson Welles decided not to run for the Senate because he thought that the voters would never elect a candidate who was a) an actor and b) divorced. Welles laughed about it in later life, but somewhere in the White House Nancy Reagan is smiling like a shark.

In the beginning, people liked to read about Hollywood divorce because it made them feel good about their own quiet lives: *he* may be handsome, *she* may be loaded but at least *I* can keep my marriage together! By the Fifties America had been vulgarized beyond belief or help by her mindless affluence, and Americans were the people we know and love today – the world's standard-bearers of bad taste and gluttony. Instead of looking at film stars' tatty private lives and feeling superior they began to feel dep-

Liz Taylor: natural wonder, natural disaster

rived, as though they had been done out of an experience they had a right to. In fact, the boy next door's divorce was so damn fascinating that it took a real hurricane of a film star to create as diverting a scandal in the screen magazines.

It took a classic comforting pattern, a pantomime in which the characters were so clear-cut that the old order was restored for five minutes between alimony payments. It took that oldest cinema scenario – the Vamp (dark, foreign), the Weak Man (hangdog, dog-eared) and the Wronged Wife (blonde, blameless). The parts could only have been written for Theda Bara, Douglas Fairbanks and Mary Pickford – or, this being the Frothy Fifties, for Elizabeth Taylor, Eddie Fisher and Debbie Reynolds.

Eddie Fisher, crooner, and Debbie Reynolds, professional cutie, married in 1955 and all of America wept like a proud mother. Eddie's weekly television show, *Coke Time* – which these days would be a drug advice forum but in those days was a Muzak show sponsored by Coca Cola – had a huge audience. Debbie Reynolds was *Tammy*, tamest teenager in captivity. There was something very small-scale about them, and they were perfect for the new paranoid Cold War America – domestic rather than dashing and definitely not dangerous. It was a marriage made if not in heaven then in the MGM publicity department.

Enter Stage Left Elizabeth Taylor (boo, hiss!). Like King Kong and Fay Wray in reverse, the larger-than-life Taylor picked up Eddie Fisher in her huge silky paw and, wriggle as he might, the Coca Cola Kid never stood a chance.

Elizabeth Taylor was newly widowed by the most charismatic all-round nothing ever to live, Mike Todd. No one could quite put their finger on what he did but he was always busy putting his finger into some pie. When he crashed and died in his private plane, 'Lucky Liz', he was masquerading as a producer of cinema epics. He had never owned a house and in the year before he died had spent a cool one and a half million dollars on nothing in particular.

Todd had been the biggest thing ever in the life of Elizabeth Taylor; she had this in common with Eddie Fisher, who heroized Todd to the extent of landing his small son (he and Debbie had one of each, to make the marriage more pukingly perfect) with the gnome-like name Todd Fisher. His death drew them together – which was bad enough – but then they started to spend evenings in, which is worse, and finally they spent as much time together as a miser and his money-belt. Mike Todd would have howled at the healthy vulgarity of it but America was not amused. Until Debbie Reynolds accepted the inevitable – that Liz Taylor was irresistible – and filed for divorce in 1958, Taylor and Fisher were so outcast and despised that they could not even go for a ride in a car: when they stopped at traffic lights people would spit and shout and swear. NBC cancelled Fisher's show and Elizabeth Taylor found herself in the surreal position of having to pay alimony to Debbie Reynolds.

This story was broken by the gossip columnist Hedda Hopper, who called Taylor to tell her off about the Fisher-filled rumours about town and no doubt expected to find the same pliable child that she and MGM had led firmly through a decade and a half of stardom and two marriages. But Taylor had been toughened up by Todd and no doubt put straight by him as to how much power a columnist actually had. So when Hopper got going, Taylor retorted, 'What do you expect me to do? Sleep alone?'

Hopper was hopping mad. Having not had it away for twenty-five years by this point, sleeping alone was exactly what she expected Taylor to do. Taylor's lack of caution or creeping politeness was what really startled her, though; the end was in sight for those Hollywood muckmongers who were legends in their own by-lines.

In the Thirties when Hays' Production Code semi-springcleaned the contents of films and the morals of the muses, he also spread his sanctions to fan magazines. Innuendo took the place of straight scandal and the mysterious Mr X and Miss Y made their first appearances. Nobody did this better than Louella Parsons, the veteran Hearst journalist, but by the end of the Thirties her rule was challenged by Hopper, a radio broadcaster. The rivalry between them produced a brand of reporting that S.J. Perelman called 'sugar and strychnine'. To get a mention in their columns became an obsession with the studios, who forced stars great and small to make a nightly round of clubs where one of the two human megaphones would be well-oiled and susceptible to flattery, despite 7am shooting schedules. Actors and actresses who had absolutely nothing in common, and who barely said a word when the camera was not on them, were forced to laugh at each other's *bon mots* and slog away at being *bon ton* when Hedda or Lolly drew near. Their all-seeing eyes probably caused many stars to marry when all they really wanted to do was screw and move on, another good reason for the divorce score that Hollywood racked up.

Lolly and Hedda were disregarded more and more as the introverted East Coast actors ambled into and annexed Hollywood – one can hardly picture James Dean putting on his best collar and cuffs and flattening his hair with water to go and knock on Hedda's door for the traditional afternoon cream tea and sympathy. By 1955 Hopper and Parsons were confined to making personal remarks about starlets' grooming; Hopper, for instance, said that Joan Collins 'looks as though she combs her hair with an egg

Judy Garland: somewhere before the rainbow-coloured pills

Pier Angeli: sad spitfire

beater.' The new popular columnists were people like the ravishing ex-GI Joe Hyams and the sexy ex-girlfriend of the elderly F. Scott Fitzgerald, London-born Sheilah Graham. They told the public the straight facts and fancies of the stars – Joe Hyams was particularly close to Taylor and Todd – rather than insinuating sin. They did not abuse their power – this would have been difficult because they had no power. Hollywood women lost their power on the printed page the same time as they lost it on the screen.

Death. Although the dreaded two-headed Lolly-Hedda monster was feared as a fire-breathing, career-burning inferno, no one ever actually took the escape route to that great film lot in the sky because Hedda-Lolly didn't take a shine to them. This was practically the only thing an actress *wouldn't* commit suicide about.

She would die for love or lack of it. She would die because she was young or because she was old. Most shocking of all in Success City, she would die for success or failure.

That white sign squatting on the Hills – in need of a new paint job until Alice Cooper recently paid for one – a decayed-toothed Sphinx's secret, standing amidst beer bottles and contraceptives as human garbage attempt to conquer a conqueror by leaving their calling card, their stain on it – is a teen idol built to last a thousand years, and teen idols attract a notoriously unstable crowd. Young girls with their family ties cut and their roots denied, believing completely in the siren's unsung song, prone to hysteria and despair. The toll of the casualties of failure – apart from the sad starlet Peg Entwhistle, who made a name for herself at last when she jumped to her death from the Hollywood Sign – is unrecorded: those girls were just the mincemeat of the factory, the sausages of suicide.

The fillet cuts of death, however, have been documented and drooled over time and time again. Fame is no sanctuary from the passing of youth, the new crop of starlets about town, the facial defects blown up to the size of a church. Suicide is much easier and more acceptable in Hollywood than growing old gracefully.

Margaret Sullavan, Jean Seberg, Inger Stevens, Marilyn Monroe and Judy Garland took sleeping pills. Pier Angeli took sleeping pills because she auditioned for a part in *The Godfather* and was told 'too old' – the female roles would later go to non-Italians such as Diane Keaton, Talia Shire and Mariana Hill. Lupe Velex took sleeping pills because she was pregnant and unmarried in Forties Hollywood. Dorothy Dandridge, glorious *Carmen Jones*, found success wanting and killed herself with sleeping pills and alcohol.

Zanuck's last protégée Bella Darvi gassed herself in Monte Carlo. Joan Dowling gassed herself in London. Thelma Todd died of carbon monoxide poisoning in her garaged car. Rachel Roberts poisoned herself. Allison Hayes died of blood poisoning. Barbara Bates put a pillow over her face and died of asphyxiation. Nancy Carroll was found dead kneeling in front of her TV set. Carole Landis slashed her wrists because Rex Harrison would not marry her.

As the dream turned sour for these women, the dream of the American male – giving it to the sex symbol up there on the silver screen – became a nightmare for Jean Harlow's husband, the young agent Paul Bern. He bled to death after performing amateur amputation on his sex organ due to his shame of impotence. This incident was thoughtfully revived by the refined Harold Robbins in his book *The Carpetbaggers* when the husband of film star 'Rina Marlowe' (guess who?) – played by Carroll Baker who just coincidentally played the title role in *Harlow* (guess who?) – commits the same act of gross indecency for the same reason.

Even those actresses who died 'natural' deaths died of horrifying diseases – emphysema, Bright's Disease, tuberculosis, multiple sclerosis, pneumonia, with a terrible tendency towards leukaemia and various forms of cancer. Many, too many to be laughed off as a coincidence, died of diseases that attack the heart and the brain – the two things an ideal film star was thought too shallow to possess. In the grey area between suicide and Act of God there were those who seemed to be victims of the fast and drastic life Hollywood let loose on them. Linda Darnell died in a fire at her home; Veronica Lake, Peggie Castle, Susan Shaw and Gail Russell died of drink; Françoise Dorleac, Jayne Mansfield and Belinda Lee died in car crashes; June Thorburn died in a plane crash; Maria Montez drowned in her bath and Natalie Wood drowned in the Atlantic while drunk. Out of all these lonely endings only one noble death came: lovely Carole Lombard who died in a plane crash while selling War Bonds. It might say something that the only film star I can think of who has died a peaceful death is Mae West – the only truly autonomous woman ever to hit the screen.

Although women die like flies in Hollywood it is men who tend to be murdered there. William Desmond Taylor's death had practically started Hollywood scandal, and the last era of scandal, the Fifties, was rounded off nicely by the death of Johnny Stompanato.

After four husbands, an old film star's fancy turns to gigolos. Johnny Stompanato was a mobster bodyguard and a 'dancing partner' – which meant he escorted wealthy and unintelligent women who would repay him all the money he spent on them in public, plus a service charge. Lana Turner was the best he had done so far – and he was the worst she had ever done.

In 1958 she made a film with the hunky British actor Sean Connery; they took a few metaphorical spins on his Vespa but the affair was wildly exaggerated by the London tabloids. 'The Battle Of The T-shirt vs The Sweater,' they swooned. On hearing the rumours, Stompanato borrowed the plane fare from the gangster Mickey Cohen and caught a flight to

Natalie Wood: a face full of fun, a bathroom cabinet full of mood-altering drugs

London. After seeing Connery, Stompanato decided not to fight him. He contented himself with generally playing up around the set until he was told to stay away. To console himself, Stompanato started knocking Miss Turner around in the privacy of suite sweet suite. Eventually she had him deported. When he turned up at her Hollywood home after her return to America the first threat had not left his lips before Turner's thirteen-year-old daughter Cheryl Crane stuck a butcher's knife into his abdomen. Like all the best Hollywood stories, there was a happy ending; Stompanato died and the heroic Miss Crane walked from the court a free teenager.

In the Sixties, film actors and actresses were accepted as people who fought and fussed and fumed and fell over drunk just like anyone else: if everyone does it then no one can get noticed doing it. It took a murder to make a noise that shook a nation – the California screaming of the sweet, foolishly malleable, gorgeous Sharon Tate Polanski in the Cielo Drive slaughterhouse. Her murder by a gang of cowardly cretins did not strictly qualify as a scandal – there was no hint of sex and the girl was eight months pregnant, which made her an honorary mother and as such worthy of respect – but the subsequent discovery of videotapes made by the mucky-minded Mr Polanski and featuring his wife, black magic, kinky boots and drugs of various descriptions made sure that Sharon Tate did not rest in peace.

In the Seventies there was a brief cocaine craze and convictions were pinned on Mackenzie Phillips (*American Graffiti*), Louise Lasser (ex-Mrs Woody Allen and ex-*Mary Hartman, Mary Hartman*), and Linda Blair of *Exorcist* and emerald-green vomit fame, but these are hardly giants of the screen. The capital of scandal is no longer Hollywood but Washington DC – Elizabeth Ray, Fanne Fox and the silly old men they embarrassed, and of course those ghastly golden Kennedys and the revelations of Joan Hitchcock and Judith Exner – that the President liked to watch girls, that he was quick as a rabbit, that he had slept with Mafia molls. In a campaign of persecution that recalls that of Ingrid Bergman, Miss Exner was called in front of a Senate Committee and subjected to harassment that bordered on terrorism by the FBI. She didn't even get a screen test out of it.

Chapter Four
THE BLEEDING HEART OF THE SCREEN DREAM

See that girl?

With the marcelled hair and the sequinned dress and the hourglass body – the Sex Express?

Why does she have a bleeding heart? I can understand it at the start. But now the girl's a big success – why is the blood running down her dress?

American propaganda has always had it that anything Left of the Daughters of the American Revolution is the yell of envy, resentment and drabness. Yet time and time again, from Marilyn Monroe – 'Communists are for the people, aren't they?' – to Jane Fonda – 'If you knew what Communism was you would pray on your knees that America would one day become Communist' – the *film star* (that job description which epitomizes all that is the apex of success and sparkle, Stateside-style), in defiance of the Road Safety rules, will look left, look right and finally look left again, defying the big wheels who want to run her down.

Why did these dream girls direct their feet to the subversive side of the street? Well, Hollywood has always been a coalition of dictators and liberals; the dictators tend to be the directors and studio heads (Harry Cohn, when Louis B. Mayer asked him for a contribution to Jewish Relief, complained to an aide when Mayer was out of earshot, 'Relief for the Jews! Somebody should start an organization for relief *from* the Jews!' – a particularly sickening statement when one considers that this was said during the War, when Hitler was mounting his own campaign for relief from the Jews), the men who gave the orders, while the liberals were the writers and actors – those who, despite their creativity, were at the bottom of the Hollywood pile in terms of being bought and sold, hired and fired. The horror of Hollywood, the gory – MONEY SEX DEATH – which is the flip-side of the glory – HARLOW GARBO MONROE – is its magnification of cap-

Jane Fonda: barefaced in the park

italism, where the people at the bottom want work so badly that the people at the top can do practically anything with them. If you're a secretary and your boss won't stop bothering you, you can find another office. If you're a pretty shopgirl and you age you'll get moved from the cosmetic counter to the dry goods depot. But there was only one Hollywood and you had to live within its pitiless city limits — it was bound to make you mad, or dead, or Red.

There were deviants, of course, all dressed up and making dates with the merchants of death — Ann-Margret said of the murderous geeks who fought the King Cong, 'I was proud to be in the same generation as those men.' Jayne Mansfield, in her pathetic bid to clone Monroe, entertained troops in Vietnam as Marilyn in a more innocent age had entertained troops in Korea, and Mamie van Doren appeared for C.R.E.E.P., the campaign to re-elect Nixon. But these are the Little Leaguers, the stuff that fish and chip folders are made of — the legends and their men (Lombard and Gable, Hayworth and Welles, Gardner and Sinatra, Bacall and Bogart, Monroe and Miller) were always liberal because they came from the poor people, and in their hearts they were poor all their lives, singing for their supper, dancing for their dinner and breaking their backs for their breakfast, idols of the innocent and serfs of the studios.

When was the first liberal spotted in Hollywood? Sometime in the early Thirties, in the vanguard of the reluctant American anti-Fascist movement.

By 1935 a good many talented trouble-makers had been taken to the bosoms of the big studios because it was then that Warner Brothers adopted the slogan 'good films – good citizenship' and began to film the lives of social achievers such as Pasteur and Zola. They were successful, and this encouraged Warners to allow their writers to take up factual themes that were not hidden in the wide berth of history – strikes and strike-breaking, lynching, slums and sharecropping. Audiences liked them but rulers and reactionaries were set, as they always are, to be scared. To them, the job of the cinema was to *divert*, not inform. 'When I want to send a message I use Western Union' was a common crack and the editor of the *Motion Picture Herald* fumed, 'If they want to preach a sermon, let them hire a hall.' Jack Warner would later appear before the Hollywood witch-hunt junta to hear his brave and buoyant films described by mental mid-gets as 'Communist-inspired propaganda' – all for the awful, awful sin of politely suggesting on celluloid that the working man deserved to have a dollar in his pocket and soles in his shoes. Even when operating in Hollywood, with the eyes of the world on them and when you would think they would be on their best behaviour, the hysteria and hypocrisy of the men who rule America knows no bounds.

But these sad days are a World War away and Hollywood is high as a kite as it escapes the clutches of the Biblical epic and jumps into the troubled but teeming-with-life twentieth century. At first these films are too new to risk stars on and women's roles are left undeveloped – all that is required of them is to witter and wail in the background, preferably clutching a healthy Hollywood baby carefully made up to look consumptive. But the public will always want girls on film, and with the onset of the Spanish Civil War came the first *showy*, socially conscious film, *Blockade* – Hank Fonda giving the glad eye to Madeleine Carroll, Hollywood's numero uno British hot property, amidst the rubble of Madrid. The lotus-eaters of California were ironically the first Americans to smell the stink of European Fascism, and actors, writers and directors rushed to join committees to send ambulances to Spain (the majestic and magnificent Gypsy Rose Lee stripteased for the Republican war effort), food to China and boycott German and Japanese imports. Yet on the eve of War, Congress was investigating Hollywood for 'warmongering'.

America was at last in the War, where it belonged, whether the cowardly Congressmen liked it or not. The top box-office attraction of 1942 was *Mrs Miniver* – Greer Garson as a British Belle braving the Blitz and bad servants, and in 1943 *Hitler's Children* showcased Bonita Granville being flogged for refusing to make sweet music with an Aryan *ubermensch*. One hundred members of the Screen Writers Guild were in the Signal Corps; Gable, Power and Fonda were in uniform. Knowledge of the European partisan girls was yet to come, and women in the West were considered fragile flowers and floosies to be stored well away from the battlefields. But even in storage they did what they could.

The teenage war-bride Norma Jean Dougherty worked in a parachute factory, waiting not for her husband but for Marilyn Monroe. Starlets posed overtime as pin-uppable tonics for the troops. Rita Hayworth met Orson Welles at a dinner party and to win his love immediately volunteered to act as an usherette at the magic show that Welles was operating for the entertainment of servicemen – she also toured New York City in the company of a soldier, a sailor, a marine and a coastguard to boost recruitment. Dietrich sang and Lombard sold. Ann Sheridan stood in the jungle telling jokes. Bette Davis organized the Hollywood Canteen with Jules Styne and every studio was assigned a night on which to supply entertainment.

Hollywood's mass mobilization against Fascism was not first blood as far as the altruistic actor's heart was concerned. In the Twenties, the young Mae West wrote and starred in a stage play called simply and splendidly *SEX*. She got thrown in jail on an obscenity charge – ten days, with two days off for 'being good'! As if such a thing were possible for Mae West! Naturally, the warder fell in love with her and let her keep her silk underwear, but Miss West was horrified at the conditions in which the other women – junkies and jades – were corralled. 'They were only given one dollar sixty to go back to the world – what chance did they have?'

Mae West wrote a series of articles about her experiences in jail – one of them made $1,200 – and donated the dough to the girls. (A further example of a movie star's caged kindness came about four decades later when Sue 'Lolita' Lyon became a prison visitor, married a black villain and became the mother of a gorgeous nymphet.)

So it was not the first blood – but it was the first from America's Achilles' artery. America's feelings of failure about the War, and about its delayed and diminutive role in it, came to the surface just two years after the War had ended, when Congressman J. Parnell Thomas opened up and brandished the can of worms called the House Un-American Activities Committee. Terrified by the strength and endurance Russia had displayed during the War, ashamed and scared that Roosevelt had had to resort to the socialistic New Deal to prop up America's crippled capitalism, America retreated into that most brutal and blundering of its hiding places – *Americanism*. Anything American was good and anything Un-American (by definition the rest of the world) was bad, bordering on evil if liberally inclined. At first Congress was content merely to trample over Roosevelt's grave, jailing his Yalta aide Alger Hiss and electrocuting the Rosenbergs (that bleeding heart, the young Brigitte Bardot, sped through Paris in a sports car scattering 'Free the Rosenbergs!' leaflets), and suggesting that every unit of the Roosevelt administration had had a hotline to the Kremlin, but finally it decided that the Second World War itself had been a

Starlets prefer spies: BB – Before Bleach – did her bit for the Rosenbergs

Mr Reagan and mate proudly present their firstborn to the world's press

perversion, mainly because it could never be right to fight on Russia's side. One of the main culprits guilty of hijacking America into war, Congress decided, had been Hollywood, so foreign and fancy out there in the sun. Hearings were established in Southern California. Cringing cowards such as Ronald Reagan and Walt Disney played ball and told all – who had asked them for a contribution to help Spanish refugees, who had been saying Hitler was a monster before America was in the War. These people, in America's neurotic eyes, were indisputably Communists, and none were redder in the House's eyes than the Hollywood Ten, a group of writers and directors who threw the Fifth Amendment of the American Bill of Rights in the face of the inquisitor. The Fifth Amendment is the right not to testify against yourself; and the Hollywood Ten were imprisoned.

Hollywood felt its foreignness. Studio heads were appalled at how violent and unpredictable mid-West maniac morality could get and visualized themselves and their hard-won goods and chattels being marched off to the dungeons and done away with. They were not brave men, so they imposed the blacklist on themselves as they had imposed the Hays Office – sacking those of their writing and directing staff who were the most liberal and, incidentally, the most talented. Hollywood's decline started *here*.

Some people were just too superior to be scared, too box-office to be browbeaten and at the Gershwins' house the Committee for the Fifth Amendment was founded – Bogart, Garland, Kaye, Kelly, Lancaster, Robinson, Wyler, Wilder, Huston, Dunne and Kurnitz. Their leader was that sterling siren Lauren Bacall Bogart (it is a *cri de coeur* and no coincidence

The Bogart-Bacalls put their best (left) feet forward for the Hollywood Ten

that the two female film stars who gave their men *their* politics rather than taking them were Jewish girls – Bacall and Shelley Winters – who grew up in the Thirties) and there were five hundred famous names on the petition she took to Washington on the plane 'Red Star', accompanied by Bogart, Danny Kaye, John Huston, the Gershwins, Gene Kelly, John Garfield and 'Baby' June Havoc, Gypsy Rose Lee's younger sister. This *corps d'élite* presented their petition, made speeches, wrote newspaper articles, lobbied senators and tried to see President Truman.

He would not see them; but the House Un-American heard them and retreated as hastily as any other playground bully does when stood up to. The House had said 'Boo!' to a few young and idealistic screenwriters and found itself faced with a Bogart, a Kelly, a Garland, a face on a million walls and a keyholder to a million hearts.

The interest span of the American people is minute and only lasts a minute and the Hollywood witch-hunts might have stumbled off sulkily into the sunset here if not for two things, two giant motifs of the Fifties – the war waged by America to save Korea from Koreans and Senator Joe McCarthy.

With a war against Communism going on abroad, subversion at home took on a whole new nerve-racking meaning. American liberals were seen as some kind of Korean Fifth Column and really not worth wasting mercy on. McCarthy had been elected as Senator for Wisconsin in 1946 but his career really started with the war, in 1950. He was from the poor and he had access to the dark superstitions of the poor – not the noble organized poor of Warner's films but the ignorant, ignoble poor who bought Hearst newspapers. He knew their massive fears and meagre dreams and he knew it was *their* sons who were being sent off to be killed by Korean Communists. He and the American scared embarked on a honeymoon spree of paranoia that was to last four years. First he saw 205 Communists in the State Department; then he said, 'The entire film industry is rife with Communism.' The HUAC was given a whiff of oxygen and this time there was no 'Red Star' or star raid on Washington – the glamorosi (Ava Gardner, Myrna Loy, Veronica Lake, Marlene Dietrich, Lauren Bacall, who dreamed of him, and Shelley Winters, who did more than dream) were out East campaigning for beloved egghead Adlai Stevenson. McCarthy marched and the crowds cheered as the destruction of careers and lives became a spectator sport.

That done, McCarthy turned his mouth on Broadway, Britain (he urged the US Navy to sink all British ships trading with China) and eventually on the US Army – an act of excruciating political suicide.

The Army vs McCarthy hearings were televised in 1954 and were watched by twenty million people. It is a fair bet that none of them, not even the most rabid Red-watcher, was on McCarthy's side when he alleged that the American Army was full of Communist commissars. McCarthy had finally gone over the borderline from inanity to insanity and for thirty-four days America watched as he put on a display of giggling, belligerent hysteria and attempted to prove that the pongos were pinko. His charges were found to be fiction and the Senate voted him as bringing the Senate into dishonour and disrepute – 67 to 22. He tried to drown his sorrows in drink but they were practised swimmers and he was forever stumbling in and out of the Senate in a trance and a suit two sizes too big. He entered Bethesda Naval Hospital in 1957, too drunk to stand or speak, and died the day after May Day. His death was the last nail in the coffin of organized Communist witch-hunts. The previous year, the skeleton of the HUAC had toyed with Arthur Miller who was seeking a passport for a trip to Britain, telling him that he was a Communist and that they might think of giving him a passport if they could have their picture taken with his fiancée Marilyn Monroe. Miss Monroe refused to pander to their end-of-the-pier fantasies and the passport was issued anyway.

Around this time, Marilyn Monroe was taking another route through the road-map of the bleeding heart, a route which has been chosen surprisingly often by film stars: she was taking instruction in a bid to convert to Judaism. Jayne Mansfield would rush to catch up in the early Sixties but the most serious searcher was Elizabeth Taylor, who converted in 1959. No

Marilyn Monroe and Arthur Miller: not waving but drowning

throwaway lines à la Ava Gardner – 'I'm a Spanish Jew from Carolina!' – for her. Elizabeth Taylor received the new name Elisheba Rachel and bought a hundred thousand dollars' worth of bonds for Israel which caused her films to be banned for ever all through the large and lucrative Arab market. Her answer to questions as to why she would wish to desert Christian Science (coincidentally Marilyn Monroe's belief before Judaism) for this religion of refugees was searingly stark – 'I feel as if I have been a Jew all my life.'

Elizabeth Taylor's humanitarianism has always been outglowed by the rings on her fingers and by her public image: the huntress in Harry Winston's. Yet when she and Richard Burton adopted a child it was a small German orphan, Maria, whose legs were so badly twisted that they faced each other. After numerous expensive operations her legs are straight; she is beautiful, a model, and resembles the young Elizabeth Taylor much more than Miss Taylor's natural children do.

While Elizabeth Taylor was converting to the oldest faith, the rest of the movie municipality was converting, it seemed, to the newest – Kennedyism. The dowdy Eisenhowers were evicted from the White House by that bronzed, brilliant, bitchy caravan with wheels of steel: Hurricane Kennedy goes to Washington! Dietrich, Winters, Loy, Lake and Joanne Woodward campaigned for him; he put his hand up Marilyn Monroe's dress and did much more to poor unstable Gene Tierney. He was a sweet if not smart man, an inspiring if not integrity-ridden leader, and to the legions of film stars he seemed like salvation – he looked like film stars used to look. These days actors spend decades and dubloons in analysis and gyms trying to get back that expensive glow that Kennedy gave away free to his celebrated camp followers.

John F. Kennedy was the bridge between the Cold War and the Hot Conflict, between keeping the enemy at continent's length and fighting them on the college campuses. The yellow enemy was joined by the young enemy: rich, pretty and educated Americans who saw through the great American lie – the one about being the policeman of the world – and laid bare the great American truth – that America is the vandal of the world. America's horrified discovery of its true nature, that of a nation based on genocide which had been hidden for two hundred years, is blown up as big as the kiss in A Place In The Sun (one in a long line of American tragedies) in the person of one rich, pretty and educated girl, Jane Fonda.

It is Jane Fonda who springs to mind, brandishing a bayonet stained with GI blood, when one thinks of a Political Film Star. Yet the girl who makes Lauren Bacall look like a floating voter started out in the early Sixties as Miss Army Recruitment, her All-American thoroughbred legs leading on unknown numbers of unknown soldiers to get shipped to Saigon. At first her interest in America's latest dirty little war in the late Sixties seemed just like the latest episode in Fonda's extended adolescence and her attempts to get Daddy to notice her. To walk the streets of a country that is receiving saturation bombing (the Americans dropped more bombs in Vietnam than were dropped by all sides during the Second World War) however, is beyond a joke or a jape or even a call for attention; it is a belief that gives rise to such bravery, and only a belief. Before returning to America from Hanoi in 1972, Jane Fonda had cooked more metaphorical geese than the US on Thanksgiving Day.

She broadcast over Vietcong radio branding the men in the Pentagon as war criminals and posed for photographs at the controls of an anti-aircraft gun which had shot down American planes. Had Ho Chi Minh not died in 1969, Jane Fonda would probably have kissed his ring. When she returned Congressmen consulted with the Justice Department on convicting her of treason – they were never given the chance to try, due to the incredible fact that Vietnam was never legally declared a war.

America was appalled when other actresses previously tolerated only as bodies and bimbos spoke out – the lovely starlet Tuesday Weld and the TV actress Susan Saint James (Miss Saint James in particular felt so strongly about American atrocities in Vietnam that, after the war was over and Fonda was attempting to reconcile maimed and injured ex-GIs with

Tuesday Weld: King Cong pin-up

the wrong they had done, she refused Fonda's offers of introduction to repentant GIs on the grounds that she would be unable to speak civilly to them).

When the Vietnam War ended in 1973, many young people who had been radical for the duration dropped back in and gave up. Jane Fonda might have followed this route had her life not already been entangled with that of Tom Hayden, the ageing student radical and ex-member of the celebrated Red Family Commune (he had been denounced and expelled for the blood-chilling crime of 'manipulative élitism', which means in English that he stirred it up amongst his comrades so he could divide and rule them). He and Fonda returned to Hollywood and huddled together being bold and bolshy; when the GIs told tall tales of torture, the two-headed Red Beast called them 'liars and hypocrites'. They were married – a marriage made in the hell of Hanoi. Jane Fonda was hardly America's sweetheart in that year of defeat, and her period of 'resting' was a hybrid of a honeymoon and a crash-course in the history of Socialism.

In August 1974 something happened that could have been engineered by an impatient agent eager for his girl's commission – Watergate. Richard Nixon was proved a crook, Jane Fonda's politics received a second look and she went back into regular employment just as Nixon left it. Every major company offered her a big-budget script and she chose *Fun With Dick And Jane*, a tale of shop-lifting in suburbia. It was really saying something and it sold – just like the string of films since then: *Julia, Coming Home, The China Syndrome, Nine To Five*. The massive money that Fonda has made from these films has been put into Hayden's campaign to win a seat in the State legislature – he represents the wealthiest stretch of land in the nation's wealthiest state, the sand from Malibu through Beverly Hills to Venice West. Their Campaign for Economic Democracy has stage-managed the election of more than fifty assembly-men, mayors and county councillors in California. They have found a certain amount of support within otherwise square organizations such as the AFL-CIO (the trad and somewhat toothless equivalent of our TUC) and the League of Women Voters.

The Fonda Haydens never stop; when she is not filming or playing house (the Haydens are happily married, with children, and they are wisely very *visibly* married; nothing wipes away a Red past in America's eyes like a Happy Family, ask Patty Hearst) Fonda is on radio and TV talk shows, at rallies, at exercise sessions (her massively fashionable and popular 'Jane Fonda Workout Salons' – all profits to CED – started the present craze for aerobics among the rich and slack single-handed). Jane Fonda – 'Hanoi Jane' – as hated a totem as Tokyo Rose, has won. Her politics cannot be laughed off, unlike the fashionable (Mia Farrow's Vietnamese orphans); the flippant (Shirley Maclaine's high-kicking passion for China); or the fascistic (Vanessa Redgrave's Lawrentian glorification of the noble savage

Arab). Fonda is not fringe, she is triumphantly, victoriously commercial and mainstream. She makes money for socialism; she uses capitalism for her own ends, as capitalists have always done, except that her ends are *right*.

In an earlier, unhappier incarnation, Jane Fonda tried to be Brigitte Bardot, but she tired of it. Brigitte Bardot also soon tired of the public pout and as early as 1966 was shedding Svengalis and retreating into a life of dumb animals and dumber young men, making films only when she needed to. Her dramatic and raw personality lends itself naturally to flamboyant and confrontational liberal politics, and she loves to make melodramas out of her crusades. When she joined the pickets at the Billancourt film studios in Paris – looking lovely in a beret and trenchcoat – she vowed 'to fight fascism to the death.' More seriously, she received in the Sixties a demand for a contribution (£3,700 to be exact) to the fanatically right-wing OAS (Organization of the Secret Army) who were responsible for some of the worst atrocities ever to happen in the French-Algerian war. Hundreds of French personalities were threatened with violence if they did not co-operate, and hundreds paid up. Bardot sent the letter to *L'Express* with her reply: 'Moi, je ne marche pas, parce que je n'ai envie de vivre dans un pays Nazi.' I won't pay, because I have no wish to live in a Nazi country. Police were posted to protect her and her son and dogs were sent to Switzerland. But she won.

Jane Fonda pretends not to notice that Tom Hayden looks like a) a corpulent capitalist b) Roman Polanski

BB: cruising for a crusade

Sophia Loren was one of the great President Tito's closest friends during the last years of his life. Even the Chelsea Girls of the Sixties, those fab flibbertigibbets whose heads were thought to be all ironed hair and no brain, fell prey to that old red magic. Jane Asher in the early Seventies could be seen in the public gallery of the House of Commons, sunny in her summer dresses, telling nosy newsmen that she was 'particularly interested in the Labour Party.' BEAUTY AND THE BEASTS, the tabloids tittered. Julie Christie has played Monroe to doyen of dissent Duncan Campbell's Miller, forever on an anti-nuclear march. Susannah York, playing a refined Mansfield to Christie's Monroe, got into the No Nukes act rather late but is now making up for lost time.

At the start of her career Christie was called a British Bardot, but it is only really now that they have something in common — Christie supplied the narration for *The Animals' Film*, Victor Schonfeld's horrifying Animal Rights documentary. Brigitte Bardot has been called 'Madonna of the Strays' since the early Sixties due to her habit of driving unannounced to various dog pounds and loading her Rolls-Royce with dogs. Lately she is known for her efforts on behalf of the seal cubs who are annually clubbed to death by sadists with a cause, going to Strasbourg to appeal to the Council of Europe on behalf of her beloved *bébés phoques*.

Actresses as diverse as BB and Doris Day save the softest parts of their bleeding hearts for animals. Elizabeth Taylor is not happy without a large diamond, four dogs, four cats and a duck — she never housebreaks her animals and they are usually to be found sitting on a king-size bed watching TV. In the early days of her first marriage, Norma Jean amazed her husband by bringing a neighbour's cow into the house because it was raining. Early Sixties beach bunny Yvette Mimieux frequents Greenpeace boats. When his relationship with Liv Ullman was breaking up, the morbid Ingmar Bergman, wanting to do something to hurt her irretrievably, tried to bribe a friend to run over her dog. Zsa Zsa Gabor says she has been married so many times 'because when the husband doesn't like the dogs I get rid of the husband.'

Except for the sad example of silent screen siren Marie Prevost — she committed suicide and her starving pet dog ate her after several days — screen dreams seem to find in their relationships with animals what they cannot find with men — a protector who won't turn on you, a friend who won't welch off you, a fan to whom you'll always look as beautiful.

Brigitte Bardot spends so much time with animals 'because the cruelty of human beings revolts me.' That the heart of the actress is alive and bleeding in the Eighties was demonstrated when plans were announced to film the life story of the Thirties Hollywood hopeful Frances Farmer. Her story is short and shattering; her beauty and early espousement of the Method took her to Hollywood where she was given roles she could do nothing

Above
Sophia: partisan when it came to Tito

Above right
Jane Asher: like Isadora Duncan, she finally caught her Scarfe

Right
Julie Christie: from Chelsea Girl to Greenham Woman

Sissy Spacek: rhymes with 'face-ache'

with. She withdrew and drank too much. When she shouted at the judge before whom she appeared for drunken driving she was condemned to a mental hospital which made Dante's Inferno resemble Rebecca's Sunnybrook Farm. She survived there for almost two decades, and it is a shame she is now dead as she would serve as a sobering symbol for all those people in the Free West who like to act shocked and scandalized that the Soviets occasionally drop dissidents into padded cells and throw away the key. Frances Farmer's crime to America was not drunken driving, it was stepping out of line once too often. She appeared for the Spanish Civil War effort, she visited Russia, she did not suck up to the studios and she wasn't scared of swearing at a judge. She was Un-American and as such subjected to the unspeakable.

When the film *Frances* was proposed, actresses queued up to test for it – testing, actresses who were submerged under scripts! Not since Scarlett O'Hara – as much an American lie as Farmer was an American truth – had so many stars acted like starlets in their haste to make themselves available to scrutiny. Jane Fonda and Tuesday Weld, Sissy Spacek and the late Natalie

Goldie Hawn: from body-painted butt of jokes to Chairman of the Board

Jessica Lange: Farmer's friend and Shepard's delight

Wood, Goldie Hawn, Valerie Perrine and Lauren Hutton – seven hearts all present, correct and bleeding. Fonda and Weld were anti-War activists, Spacek and Wood were of Russian descent, Goldie Hawn is a Jewish girl and Hutton was a model, Perrine a showgirl – five Un-Americans and two members of the dumb professions, ideal idealistic victims! The part – which without doubt should have gone to Tuesday Weld, who would have been perfection – finally went to Jessica Lange, whose experience of persecution starts and ends with being picked up and kissed by the big ape in the awful remake of *King Kong*.

Those hearts start bleeding early these days: Brooke Shields says 'animals are my oxygen' and speaks sharply of Vienna Zoo, where the cages are too small for her liking; Charlene Tilton, the miniature Mae West of *Dallas*, can be seen on picket lines during actors' strikes – 'just supporting my union, honey!' – while Pamela Sue Martin takes a year off between *Playboy* centre-folds and marrying a millionaire to go off on that slow boat to Newfoundland with Greenpeace. Young hearts run free – and never stop bleeding.

Chapter Five
CHELSEA GIRLS

Who toppled the Sex Doll as the supreme celluloid sex-dream? The Chelsea Girl! Did the creature behind the boots and the fringe and the eyelashes have ancestors? Maybe Holly Golightly, who came from nowhere; maybe Brigitte Bardot in *And God Created Woman*, who was a victor and not a victim when it came to sex; maybe Juliette Greco and the Left Bank beat girls who drifted from day to day, from dream to dream.

Who was the Chelsea Girl? On film she was Julie Christie and Jane Birkin and Judy Geeson, but these were merely nicely-spoken, semi-precious gems, shadows of the original rough diamond, the Girl From Nowhere (a converted railway-carriage in a Slough gravel pit) who knew Everyone (Russians, Tories, refugees) – Christine Keeler. Her story is the story of how the Frothy Fifties became the Swinging Sixties, how the ideal of female beauty moved from Hollywood to London.

There was something for everyone in the Profumo Affair – sex for the starved, capitalist decay for the Communists, beauty for the beasts. For the youth – proof. A show of strength; one girl from Slough had brought down the Conservative government of Macmillan – Supermac, provider of butter and sugar in great quantities for the first time since the War; manna to the man in the street – and left the stage squeaky clean for the first Labour government since the Forties.

Christine Keeler started the Longest Party – with all reputation gone, Britain had no stuffy standards to live up to and therefore could have the party with no holds barred. DON'T invite the neighbours! DON'T keep the noise down!

Patron of the party was Harold Wilson who in 1964 appropriately became the youngest Prime Minister of the century. He dazzled the revellers' ears with the duplicit jargon of pop science: we would all be happy when

Love on the rocks: BB in *And God Created Woman*

Juliette Greco: big in the Left Bank *boîtes*,
but cold croissants at the box office

Christine Keeler: The Girl From Nowhere at
the court of Lord Denning

'the white heat of the scientific revolution' had transformed our island 'in one hundred days of dynamic action.' He *burned* advice. He represented Liverpool, which was perfect; he marched the Beatles off to Buck Pal and made the Queen give them the MBE.

The Beatles did not start the Longest Party, but they were its roving ambassadors and they made the most money out of it. They were particularly useful in spreading the British Is Best baloney to young America, which was depressed after John Kennedy's slaughter and thirsting for a saviour or four. Within a year of Kennedy's death, America was Beatle-obsessed, and not one major crime was committed by a teenager in the whole of the US during the duration of the Beatles' first American television appearance.

Back in Britain, the gatecrashers took control of the party. There is a rather soppy, poppy way of looking at the Sixties as the first spontaneous kick-up ever. Nonsense; in the Forties, the electorate rejected Tory authority and elected a Labour Government; in the Fifties, Teddy boys went to quite violent lengths to have a good time. The Sixties were not a 'revolutionary' invasion of the upper strata by precocious proles. Rather they were a result of deliberate and skilful slumming by middle-class youth who for the first time suspected that the working-class young were having a much better time than they were.

The youth of the various classes is almost impossibly segregated. I did not meet one non-working-class person until I was sixteen and my working-class friends *still* know only their own kind. The same is broadly true of the youth of other classes. In the early Sixties, though, the experiment of class-cross-pollenation all in the cause of a good time was going on at Peter Rachman's nightclub where Princess Margaret, the Kray twins, the Duke of Kent, Michael Caine, Guards, debutantes and Terence Stamp all swanned, a hot-pot brought to light by the ripples of the Profumo Affair. Christine must have seemed the luckiest girl in the world to the bored convent-convicted daughters of the professional classes — sex, spies *and* instant celebrity.

Then there were the Mods and the massive media coverage they received — the sharpest and sweetest youth cult ever to hit the yellow press turned middle-class kiddies green. Mods were immaculately dressed children who held down a steady job all week and on a Friday night took huge doses of amphetamines (diet pills, designed to make ordinary life seem a half-life in comparison) which sent down their sex drive (thus protecting them from constrictive and corrosive shot-gun weddings) and sent their dress drive, dance drive, life drive up, up, UP. The Mods held their parties on long West End weekends, but when the rich kids gatecrashed, the party became constant because of their money. Mindful of where the party started, however, they adopted working-class slang and took what were beginning to pass for jobs so as not to appear mere flappers – they took photographs, made pop records, became models – some acted.

It seemed as though one minute Britain could do nothing and the next minute it could do nothing wrong – pop, ballet, art, theatre, especially GIRLS. Britain suddenly produced a crop of dazzlingly beautiful girls out of nowhere, just when Marilyn had died and beauties were needed – no English Roses, either, more English Thorns. They were sharp and swinging and they were *cool* – no Hollywood gush or baby-girl breathlessness – because they were based on Christine, and that was her angle – not so much a call-girl as a Cool Girl. None of them had the sex-shock she had – when you see the professional studies of Christine taken in the mid-Sixties, you see what made her so irresistible to all men: she looks *in thrall* to sex, the look that Marilyn always tried for, with her eyes half-closed, mouth half-open pose. But Marilyn's love of sex was an affectionate affectation – she was too ambitious or scared or victimized to really feel it – but they had studied her photographs well and their style suddenly made the American Sex Doll look as crass as the American flag.

The most beautiful of them were photographic models and had no desire to be anything else, which shows how the cinema had declined since Marilyn's genesis when she saw modelling as a seamy, low-status way to get noticed by the studios – Celia Hammond, Patti Boyd, Jill Kennington, Sandra Paul, Paulene Stone, Angela Howard, Susan Murray and of course Jean Shrimpton, the Face of the Sixties, and, to my mind, the Century.

Jean Shrimpton: Beauty and the Beat

Sensing that girls on film had had their day and that only dog-ends of roles were likely to be offered to beautiful girls post-po-faced-Method, Jean Shrimpton fought shy of film offers until making *Privilege* at the end of the decade. It was one of the first disaster movies in that it was a total disaster; Shrimpton was required only to trail around in the wake of some wimp turned crooner turned Messiah and look depressed. It was no mere act; the experience worried her so badly that her precious hair began to come out in handfuls and not long after she decided to quit the business of being beautiful for a living altogether. She became a photographer and now owns a Cornish hotel.

The other mega-model of the Sixties was Twiggy; less beautiful, more tough, and very gimmicky. She had been a Mod and boasted a grating Neasden accent that the Americans bought in a big way; she was the real thing – so real as to seem studied and phoney. But she was a prole, and any prole in a storm was a cause for celebration in the Sixties. Working-class girls, from whom the style had been hijacked in the first place, were thin on the ground, swamped by doctors' daughters from the Home Counties determined to grab themselves a genuine Cockney carnal trophy. There was Cathy McGowan, who wriggled and giggled on *Ready Steady Go!*; Sandie Shaw, a slant-eyed, slinky, barefoot singer whom the French loved;

Cathy McGowan: the lost weekend starts here

Sandie Shaw: new classlessness meets old contemptibles

Twiggy: living proof that you can be too thin

and the only working-class Sixties actress I can think of, Carol White, who came to a very depressing and un-swinging end in all of her films.

The somewhat sordid immorality of the working-class girl – Christine Keeler, Sandie Shaw when named and condemned as co-respondent by a divorce judge, Carol White's unhappy endings – contrasted suspiciously with the accepted swinging amorality of the middle-class Sixties screen-dream; sex with a safety net, a lady being a lady no matter how dirty she gets. Julie Christie, Judy Geeson, Jane Birkin, Charlotte Rampling, Sarah Miles, Jane Asher, Vanessa Redgrave, Suzy Kendall, Angela Scoular, Susan George, Susannah York – they all skated in and out of sex unscathed, protected by the hair-pieces and miniskirts they wore like armour against amour, riding roughshod over men's hearts and minds on the way to the next thrill – these boots are made for WALKING! Emma Peel, the TV Avenger, was the last word in this frosty fantasy female, as played by Diana Rigg in neck-to-toe black leather and all-over scepticism – a girl who'd break your back as soon as the Sex Doll would scratch it.

Emma Peel was an exception – her capacity to inflict injury was signalled by her combat clothes. The Chelsea Girl hatched her hostilities against whoever she imagined was holding her down behind the shiny façade, ruining the poor jerk in the last reel without a backward glance over the Quanted shoulder. Julie Christie did this first and best and was the period's most interesting actress.

Born in India and schooled in England, a brief spell in a bottling factory and a Lilo to sleep on and a copy of Marx's *Kapital* to carry around like old-fashioned girls carried handbags, she had all the right qualifications.

Christie travelled *light*, a Chelsea Girl necessity – her hair just *hung*, her soul just *swung*, she looked like she'd just stepped off the King's Road and in front of the camera. In 1962, she walked off with *Billy Liar* as the free-wheeler who attempts to tempt the dazed day-dreamer away to a new life in London, and in 1965 she walked off with the Oscar for *Darling* and her role as the ambitious model, Diana.

Christie did not identify with her anti-heroine – she dismissed her as 'stupid' – but she did cling tight to the clichés of the day – 'I hate to age. To be young is to be beautiful.' She lived the line, too; on hitting her thirties in the Seventies, Christie took herself off to California and hibernated in luxury for a decade before the battle-cry of the crusading cinema brought her back to Britain.

Charlotte Rampling was good as bitchy and glittering prizes; Suzy Kendall was best as soft-centred swingers; Judy Geeson was a great perverse princess, her dry and defiant drone and her evasively effective non-acting often making a silk purse out of pure pigswill. In 1968's *Here We Go Round The Mulberry Bush*, she played Mary Gloucester, a sunnier younger sister of Diana Darling and a Sixties Dream Girl in her own right – always jumping

Above left
Julie Christie: replete with that distinctly Sixties ring of confidence

Above
Jane Birkin: corrupt choirboy as sex kitten

Left
Judy Geeson: born free

Angela Scoular and Barry Evans have some good clean fun in *Here We Go Round The Mulberry Bush*

into a sports car or swinging down the street in a miniskirt short enough to be a cummerbund, a perfect fringe and a fickle power. The film also featured Angela Scoular, an underrated Chelsea Girl who seemed to play every role as bedroom farce. At the time it did little to help her career but looking back at how seriously most actresses took the best and brashest bashes of their lives, her mindless modern minxes were a breath of fresh froth.

While Southern girls swang, Northern boys bellowed; films like *A Kind Of Loving* and *Saturday Night, Sunday Morning* told of the towns too trashed to party – the towns of the North of England, the ashtray of the industrial revolution. They might have been the voice of dissent that the Longest Party needed to clear stale air and give some sense of purpose – had they not been so reactionary and hysterically masculinist themselves. As if in revenge for all the girl-centred, swinging Southern movies, the only people one was encouraged to sympathize or empathize with was the belly-aching boy hero; the plight of their female counterparts was never thought worthy of unwinding even though the pressures to conform on the working-class girl are so much greater. Instead, these Northern girls invariably appear as shallow, acquisitive burdens who are happy that way – things that get pregnant and get dependent and weigh a wild working boy down when he could be out there taking on the world.

Post-War Western Europe's uprisings against the American occupier have been few but furious and mainly cultural; the rebellion of Sixties cinema was total and terrifically timed, coming when the masses who might have kept the American monolith going were getting to know their TV sets. And the Southern slickers who were left decided that while America spoke the same language in *theory*, Europe spoke it in practice and in the flea-pit. Cinemas all across the country showing Hollywood fare were at least half empty despite the lures of Cinemascope, Todd A-O, Cinerama and other gimmicky Americana – but when Alain Resnais's first film, *Hiroshima Mon Amour*, came to London in 1960 there were four shows a day, all packed, no seats bookable, the telephone always busy and, incredibly, ticket touts. Fellini's *La Dolce Vita* made the kind of money that turned All-American capitalist pigs green; Louis Malle, Claude Chabrol and Jean-Luc Godard did well. The only American in Paris/Rome/London who could hold his head up was Joseph Losey (an exile in London since the McCarthy witch-hunts) who made *The Servant* in 1963 (a milestone in eternal triangle's clothing – Sarah Miles, Dirk Bogarde and James Fox, the first a pretentious pain, the second and third proof that boys will be Chelsea Girls too given half a chance and a benevolent censor) and suggested that swinging sex was too kinky to be kind.

Mainland Europe had the directors, but there was no getting away from the fact that we had the girls – the London Look, New York gushed, le Style Anglais, Paris squealed. That's not to say that the rest of the world didn't try for the Cool Girl; real ethnic spitfires from real ethnic countries – Claudia Cardinale, Senta Berger, Virna Lisi, Elsa Martinelli – just cut their hair into

Claudia Cardinale: have fringe, will travel   Elsa Martinelli: spaghetti starlet

fringes, put on their jeans and played at being Cool. But they were too warm, apart from Monica Vitti who fell into the hands of Antonioni and walked around his lifeless landscapes mistaking comatose for Cool. The Françoises Dorleac and Hardy tried hard, but they were too much on the moody side. When American money enabled François Truffaut to make his first film in colour, it was Julie Christie he chose to play both girls in *Fahrenheit 451*.

Since Brigitte Bardot showed American men what girls looked like with their clothes off ten years earlier, Hollywood had been alerted to the commercial possibilities of European cinematic art. Art meant Bare! – the descriptions 'Art House' and 'Dirty Cinema' became one and the same in the American mind. Without soiling the skin of American girls and making a nonsense of their encrusted old Code, Hollywood companies could give a shot of sex-cash to their failing returns by distributing European films in America.

Before the War, European talent had been easy to buy from the poor Old Countries: Garbo, Bergman, Dietrich, Lubitsch, Lamarr, Leigh, Chaplin, Olivier. The trend had continued into the Fifties with the exodus of Italian girls. But in the Sixties, America – killing Vietnamese, killing Kennedys, killing King, not so much a country as a way of killing – was not the place to be and there was no tune that America had the gall to call. In 1966, Antonioni refused to let MGM – *MGM* – make the cuts required by the Motion Picture Production Code in *Blow-up*, the condemnation of Swinging London and its inmates that the old codgers of the Code obviously thought looked like fun and might inspire every American girl to take off her clothes and roll on the floor with the nearest available photographer. The studio released it without the Code's seal of approval under the name of one of their subsidiaries and this practice was soon widespread. Hollywood had become a prize ponce.

It was clear that the Day of Doris was gone for ever and that the market to put your mark on was the youth market. Where cinemas and films were losing money, drive-ins and Elvis Presley's string of cinematic stinkers – twenty-five in a decade, all made dirt-cheap and raking in around five million dollars a throw – were making wise men filthy rich. Old Hollywood was looking more like a museum every day; old concepts of glamour were suddenly as embarrassing as a punctured falsie.

In 1965 the Beatles, the bringers of the Swinging Word to colonial outposts, gave an interview to *Playboy* magazine. The person they had most wanted to meet, they said, had been Jayne Mansfield. Well, they had met her. And now Paul McCartney said, 'She's a clot. But you won't print that anyway, of course, because *Playboy* is very pro-Mansfield. They think she's a rave. But she really is an old bag.' *Playboy*, who to that point had loved Jayne Mansfield above all women, due to her habit of disrobing at the snap of a camera-shutter, never featured or mentioned her again. They were old Americans and as such terrified of seeming prehistoric to young Britishers. Jayne Mansfield was the last gasp of Old Hollywood and the furthest thing imaginable from the clean and long and lean Chelsea Girl – she must have seemed particularly horrific to the complainant McCartney, whose girl-friend throughout the Sixties was the beautiful, orange-haired, swinging waif, Jane Asher. Mansfield was a woman of thirty-three with three failed marriages and four children behind her. She looked like a drag queen after a hard night on the tiles and she was the best Hollywood, that legendary connoisseur of flesh, had to offer.

Closer to *Ruby* than Christine when it came to Keelers, Hollywood, caught with its curlers in, was mad at Mansfield. These long-limbed, sulky, sexy baby girls of England – like the daughter you always wanted to jump on! Like a beloved beach bunny, only Oscar-winning and relevant! America grabbed the nearest young girl with straight hair and no lipstick and threw her onto the screen – Faye Dunaway, Katharine Ross, Ali MacGraw, Karen Black, Candice Bergen, Jennifer O'Neill, Sally Kellerman, Barbara Hershey, Stefanie Powers and anybody else who could prove she had never had a facelift or a baby. Unfortunately, they were the most boring bunch ever to bend your ear in a bus queue.

American girls could never do Cool properly – they thought it meant standing about looking blank when of course it meant always giving the impression of imminent *movement* while standing perfectly still. The

Ali MacGraw: Where do I begin/ To tell the story of how dull a girl can be?

Katharine Ross: in her films, wide-eyed and brainless, she was the human duvet – always warm and waiting for her man

Candice Bergen: they didn't call her Charlie McCarthy's sister for nothing

British girls *were* stars, although not built along traditional hour-glass lines – Dunaway, Ross and all were nice-looking girls with chiselled if boring features and would have made good photographic models. The British girls were linked to the film stars of the past in that their faces had at least one great feature which was constantly used, which trapped your eyes. Christie had a huge, beautiful mouth; Rampling had singularly corrupt eyes and Geeson had both. Eyes and mouth are essentially the stuff that sex goddesses are made of – Loren's nose was long and Monroe's legs were short but they both had eyes that spellbound and a mouth that men wanted to hold down, capture and crush.

Any man of the era that these floundering American girls played against – Warren Beatty, Dustin Hoffman, Steve McQueen, Robert Redford, Paul Newman, Jon Voight – not surprisingly swamped them and was eventually whisked off to play opposite another man. It is reasonable to suspect that this had been a desired end all along; despite the generally unisex feel of the decade, Sixties Hollywood after the springclean was a man's world. In their efforts to reject all that Old Hollywood held dear, the movie brats threw out the 'woman's film', the 'woman's director' and eventually the woman herself. The New Hollywood prided itself on being anti-star, and actresses were irretrievably bound up with the studio star system in a way that a few men – Clift, Dean, Brando – had given the impression of avoiding. Therefore actresses must be taken down a peg or two.

It seems impossible that the Sixties was the time of feminist breakthrough in America when one compares the celluloid evidence with that of the Thirties. See Harlow and West wise-cracking their way through life; see Garbo and Dietrich use the world as their stage. Gape disbelievingly at the almost impossibly underdeveloped characters that, say, Katharine Ross is called upon to sleepwalk through in *Butch Cassidy And The Sundance Kid* and *The Graduate* – women who wait, and are grateful to.

Fear of strength-sapping Communists decimated the Old Hollywood and fear of strength-sapping goddesses made sure that the New Hollywood would go from weakness to weakness to the ghost town it is now. What a way to end the Longest Party!

Whatever happened to the Girl From Nowhere, the catalyst of Cool herself? Well, in the mid-Sixties an American film producer planned to make a movie called *The Keeler Affair* starring the girl. Wouldn't you know, she was dropped and only spoke the introduction on the finished product – there were vague and veiled orgies, it was barely shown and badly received. What a waste! Had it been the Thirties, the girl would have been whisked away to the shelter of the Sign and would probably be walking a leopard on a leash down Sunset Boulevard! Still, at least she went to Cannes...

Chapter Six
GRINGOS PREFER BRUNETTES

It is typically silly Oscar Wilde to say that each man kills the thing he loves. What he does is legal and even more disloyal – he gets bored with it.

It was the Fifties and each man wanted a Sex Doll – but he was soon bored and by 1954 he had shipped over the gamine from Western Europe. By 1956 he had discovered the Southern European, the spitfire, the Nubile Savage. There had been pre-War Latins, South American girls who through beauty or starvation or proximity got to Hollywood. But these had varied: Dolores del Rio played pale, grave, beautiful heroines after arriving in Hollywood with a reputation of being the richest girl in Mexico and fifty thousand dollars in shawls and combs to prove it; Lupe Velez was a big success in the *Mexican Spitfire* movies; Maria Montez of the Dominican Republic and Universal Studios vamped to excess in Forties Technicolor Easterns – films which read like a listing of homosexual heaven viewing, *Cobra Woman, Gypsy Wildcat, Siren Of Atlantis* – until overtaken in the Fifties by the more homely and wholesome (and white) Yvonne de Carlo who mined the same sequinned seam; Carmen Miranda, the Brazilian Bombshell, stormed to popularity in wartime Hollywood by being hysterically happy and mindless and wearing the contents of a fruiterer's on her head. Her career now looks like a parody of condescending and cretinous US relations with Latin America (the trouble with South America is North America!) and her films read like a litany of torture and trouble hotspots – *That Night In Rio, Copacabana, Weekend In Havana, Down Argentine Way*.

The Nubile Savage had always been a useful gimmick for getting flesh into a film by having the spitfire in question indulge in spontaneous bathing in a conveniently lily-covered pool, something the artificial Sex Doll or the shy gamine would never be unselfconscious enough to do. Dolores del Rio did it in *The Gateway To Heaven* and even old Clara Bow as

Carmen Miranda: fruit salad days

a Polynesian plaything took a dip in *Hula*.

The Latin – the supposed unbridled lust of the Negress with the silky hair and classic features of the dream white girl. There wasn't the same sense of guilt and of *using* with a Latin that there might be with a Negress – so she appealed to men who were trying hard to be good guys – because for all *she* knew, you might marry her in the end. It *was* feasible that you might marry a Latin without becoming a social outcast; 'Hi, Mom, this is Luana! We just got married in Tijuana! Foreign? Heck, no – she's just got a good suntan! It'll soon wear off here in Idaho!'

A lot of Italian girls married GIs after the War, second only in volume to the brides corralled in Britain, but the attitude to Italy and all who sailed in her was ambivalent. Italy had been part of the Axis, the Enemy, and America entered it as a conqueror rather than a liberator. A GI might make a present of a bar of precious chocolate to a French girl and hope for something in return; in Italy there was no question that he could buy a girl for that, the poverty and the sense of guilt was so great. It is fair to say that the Americans treated Italy like one big bombed-out brothel, and this may be why Italy's Communist Party does such thriving business.

After war had broken their country, Italian girls seem to have utilized their beauty to survive; like Negroes box, Italian girls look sexy, both reflex action and the only thing they could rely on. Whatever, they found refuge in Hollywood, all determined to be fiery no matter how depressed they

95

felt: Lucia Bose, Miss Italy of 1947, Silvana Pampanini, Rosalina Neri, Pier Angeli, Gina Lollobrigida, Silvana Mangano who in *Bitter Rice* made underarm hair a thing of beauty – one girl, Lisa Gastoni, went to Britain instead and became a walking pin-up in Fifties comedies. Being Italian became so firmly associated with being an empty-headed spitfire that Anne Bancroft – who had been blessed with the voluptuous handle Anna Maria Italiano – changed her name when she started out in the Fifties as an Actor's Studio heavy lest directors expect her to turn up at auditions for *Hedda Gabler* with a rose between her teeth.

There was a brief flurry of interest in a variation on the spitfire: the Island Girl as played by Movita and Kerima (who undertook the longest screen kiss with Trevor Howard in *Outcast Of The Islands*), girls from islands that *vaguely – sometime, somehow – belonged to white men* – as good a description as any of the Nubile Savage's appeal. The South American still smouldered her way across the border – Katy Jurado, big in Mexican films since 1943, was brought to Hollywood in 1952 and stole *High Noon* out from under Grace Kelly's pallid patrician nose before going on to toss her hair and show her shoulders for the remainder of her hell-cat career (she was thereafter relegated to the Wise Old Crone cadre); Rita Moreno from Puerto Rico who had been in showbusiness since her Thirties childhood and in 1952 stole *The Fabulous Señorita* – she was! Her personification of

Sophia Loren: the girl who really was (almost) too beautiful

Pier Angeli: somewhere between Lauren and Loren

the singing, dancing, sizzlingly proud Anita in *West Side Story* won her an Oscar but no future; she never became a box-office attraction and the screen's loss was the floorshow's gain when Miss Moreno counterspun to cabaret.

Miss Moreno made the best spitfire yet, but this was 1961 and the pouting pitch had been queered somewhat by a Neapolitan bastard turned Olympian Other. Sophia Loren had had the typical Italian beauty's background: at fourteen she hitch-hiked to Rome with her mother, entered a beauty contest and found work as an extra. She appeared in numerous films from 1948 on until in 1956 Hollywood saw and called, seeking merely to add yet another Med minx to its roster. She made five American films in 1957 and four in 1958 – none of them even sniffed success. Nine failures in two years is a lot of let-down in any language.

Loren *looked* like the absolute last word in the evolution of the lovely Latin, but something stood between her beauty and her box-office. It was her strength, the strength she had needed to survive and now could not kiss off, even to save her career. Lou Schreiber of Twentieth Century Fox described with acerbity and accuracy why he would not employ her even if she paid him to: 'Men are frightened of her. She's too big, she's too powerful, too ballsy.' Loren was a luscious version of those other *too* ethnic actresses of the Mediterranean – the Italian Anna Magnani, the Greeks Irene Papas and Melina Mercouri, all of whom made short and unsatisfactory round trips to Hollywood – who all shared the guts that women of their origins *had* to possess to earn a crust in a country full of lazy Mediterranean men: they are so womanly they are almost manly, as Hardy described his Bathsheba.

That's why the spitfire is a sap; for all the initial kick and scratch challenge she presented to the hero she could easily be tamed in time for the credits with little more show of strength than a slap and a discreet glow of sweat on the lion-tamer's temples. The spitfire was all surface joy and tears, a parody of the white woman's illogical emotionalism, and Loren could no more act the mindless spitfire than Garbo could act the stupid, sexy Scand – Ekberg, Ekland, Ege – if she returned today. Loren's meltingly Mediterranean beauty had a stubborn calm core, a clear-eyed, clear-conscienced recall of real danger danced with, dismembered and remembered. She really was quality, a hybrid of homespun and heaven, and she made the surface shimmer of Fifties Americana look a mere cheap shininess like the seat of trousers worn too long. Nothing illustrates this more than the photographs taken at the Hollywood arrival party which Jayne Mansfield crashed and sought to steal – Loren sits at her table, dark hair, dark skin, dark dress, dark dignity, while Mansfield hangs over her soliciting the camera, the celebrated bosom resembling a brace of barrage balloons gone bust. The difference between them is the difference between silk and polyester.

What Loren did to Mansfield at a party – dwarfed her in every way possible – she was doing to men on the screen, and the problem of how to make such a natural wonder pay off was only solved by removing her from the alfresco frolics with half-wits and half-men that her colouring had condemned her to – John Wayne, Alan Ladd – and setting her against sparring partners of the first order – Clark Gable, Anthony Quinn, Anthony Perkins, Peter Finch, Gregory Peck. A star is cut loose.

Sophia Loren in her element appeals to people who do not care for film actresses, as Garbo did in her time, because she has and always has had *style*, a style which is bred in the brittle bones of the poor and never more often than among teenage black girls who, like Loren, wear cheap clothes like gold cloth. David Bailey, veteran of Jean Shrimpton and Marie Helvin, considers her to be the most beautiful woman ever; Noel Coward, not known for his love of women and certainly not known for his affection for swarthy and spicy sexpots, saw in Loren the elegance beyond sex that he saw in Marlene Dietrich, his other pet interest of the celluloid circus.

When one looks at Loren, so much meets the eye that it seems impossible that there could be more there. But in 1961 someone must have seen more because Sophia Loren received the Academy Award for Best Actress, the Best Actress Award at Cannes, the New York Drama Critics Award and the British Film Institute Best Foreign Actress Award. The magnet that turned these exalted baubles into iron filings was *Two Women*, de Sica's reading of Moravia's novel, in which the twenty-five-year-old Loren played a woman in her thirties determined to protect her teenage daughter from the afterbirth of war. She removed her make-up and she remembered Naples and the film became the graveyard of the fun-loving and fiery little fool whom every man should house-break and bend to his will for a while before beating a path to a nice blonde's door. The spitfire was revealed as a casualty of colonialism, a Displaced Person who didn't feel like dancing any more – you had seen your last samba, heard your last 'Si'.

The guilt that certain American men felt about their treatment of certain Italian girls was a suitable subject for filming as the guilt was not collective and the victim had collaborated – it was not an American Sin as such. America's treatment of Negroes, particularly the South's treatment, is a different glass of julep altogether and blacks – especially black women – are almost thought to be too volatile and dammed up with anger and remembered atrocities to let near a mixed audience. Black women have been mothers without children (Mammies – who can ever forget the sickening spectacle of Hattie McDaniels waiting on the simpering Vivien Leigh hand and foot and enquiring like a ninny, 'What's ma lamb gonna wear?' at strategic interludes?) and sex-dreams without sex – Lena Horne, the first black performer signed to a long-term contract with a major (MGM),

Sophia Loren: Neapolitan Nefertiti

Hattie McDaniels: true grits

looked gutless but was actually quite spirited. She seethed when Tallulah Bankhead complimented her on the paleness of her skin and the non-Negroidness of her features. Singing was Lena Horne's safety valve: she sang to a man when she should have been singeing him with her kisses. Dorothy Dandridge was misused in the same manner.

In the mature Forties, Hollywood decided to get to grips with the meaty and messy topic of multiracial romance, but it was a morbid business. Even when the girls were gorgeous white girls you'd be pleased to take to a KKK kafe klatsch (Jennifer Jones and Jeanne Crain, for God's sake! If they were any whiter they'd glow in the dark!), multiracial romance brought tears, traumas and suicide. The message was clear: you intelligent white men suffer enough guilt because of what your grandaddy did – you want to suffer some more? Keep away from these girls – they're the guilt on the gingerbread!

It has taken TV to showcase black actresses decently – *Roots*, with Cicely Tyson, Leslie Uggams and the glorious Irene Cara. That the cinema has never attempted to show us the ancient American South from the black's point of view while boring us to death indefinitely with the white man's myths of how picturesque, how pure, how proud it was, is forever to the cinema's shame. Still, how can you expect an American audience to pay out good money to be told the *truth*?

Baby, remember my name! Um, Jennifer Beals? No, Irene Cara

Oriental girls have never been a delicate problem, but they have been a difficult one. Are they prim or passionate? They're certainly hard to get a comfy clichéd handle on, so Hollywood has mostly steered clear of them. In the early Thirties Anna May Wong, an American of Chinese parentage, was a success on both sides of the Atlantic, usually playing villainesses. She was a shy and sweet and superstitious girl who believed that every time her gorgeous face was photographed the camera stole a part of her soul. In 1958 the breakable beauty France Nuyen was loved and left like litter by a GI cad in *South Pacific* and in 1960 the gorgeous Nancy Kwan started out by starring in *The World Of Suzie Wong* and passing the acid test that will always be the criterion beyond cranky Methods and trends that defines great acting – she could make you laugh and two minutes later make you cry. But there was no call for an Oriental angle on the white world and Nancy Kwan went on to years of wasteland such as 1975's sickeningly-named *Supercock*.

If Oriental girls were hard done by, the low visual profile of Jewish girls on screen made the average earthworm look like a high-flyer. Like no other ethnic group, Jews are not the stuff that matinée idols are made of. From all angles this is perverse. From the first vamp, Theda Bara, Jewish girls have been drawn to the movies, having the added advantage/misfortune of the Jewish Mother, who is practically interchangeable with the Stage Mother. Jews also happen to run the film industry, their only monopoly despite the Zionist Conspiracy theories that give them the banks, the newspapers, television, radio and the Universe. It could be that familiarity breeds contempt and that studio heads desire the Other as much as any other man. Whatever, when it was suggested to Harry Cohn that he groom the great Judy Holliday for stardom he said, 'You're joking! Films are made for Jews and by Jews – not WITH Jews!'

Jewish men have to play by the same rules. From Valentino to Travolta, Latin has been box-office but Jewish men become WASPs overnight in the studios' publicity departments. Asa Yoelson becomes Al Jolson, David Daniel Kaminsky becomes Danny Kaye, Julius Garfinkle becomes John Garfield, David Meyer becomes David Janssen.

Paulette Goddard was a Levy, Ethel Merman was a Zimmerman, Jill St John was an Oppenheim. Judy Tuvim became Holliday, Barbara Herzstine became Hershey, Claire Blume became Bloom. Harriet Shapiro was given the starchy East Coast society name Susan Cabot, Betty Weinstein-Bacal became Lauren the legend, Shelley Winters was born Shirley Schrift, Yvonne Mitchell was a Joseph, Lilli Palmer was a Peiser, Lizbeth Scott was really Emma Matzo, Dana Wynter was Dagmar Spencer-Marcus, Lee Grant was Lyova Rosenthal. Daliah Lavi was born Dalia Levenbuch, a native Israeli *sabra*, and in the Sixties she decorated spy spoofs as ANYTHING but an Israeli and a Jew. The only Jewish actresses who never changed their names

Claire Bloom looking like the Queen, or perhaps just a Jewish princess

were Susan Strasberg, Joan Collins and Barbra Streisand – Strasberg because of the massive respect her parents Lee and Paula had earned the name, Collins because who ever heard of a WASPier name than Joan Collins, and Streisand because she was BARBRA STREISAND.

Jews were an embarrassment because the white world is happier with images that are literally black or white. The Jews were the only ethnic group who could pass for white so pass they must, with a vengeance. The only man in Hollywood to see Jews as exotics was Marlon Brando, that one-man sexual atlas and minorities fetishist – his girls included Movita, Rita Moreno and Anna Kashfi (he married her thinking she was Indian and went mad crazy when he discovered she had tricked him – although she had grown up in India she was an Irish girl, name of Callaghan) and he sent a Red Indian model, Sasheen Littlefeather, to collect his Oscar. The only blondes he ever saw were Jewish blondes – Ellen Adler and Shelley Winters.

But Hollywood was a perverse bitch and could occasionally be found committing her favourite folly – cross-casting – upon the bodies of beautiful Jewish girls, like making Piper Laurie a Casbah spitfire and Debra Paget an eternal squaw. I can believe any feat of cultural transvestism from a town that gave Garbo her first American role as a Spanish dancer! So Lenore Ulric made her talkie debut as an Eskimo minx in *Frozen Justice*; Natalie Wood's Indian summer colouring took her through Red Indians, Jews, Italians and Puerto Ricans; Mary Stanton became Dorothy Lamour, forever bursting out of a sarong and into song as a siren of the South Sea Islands; Myrna Loy, a Welsh-American, hid beautiful silky red hair and

In the Sixties girls had thighs, even Barbra Streisand

slinky features under fright wigs and slitted eyes for a decade until she became Mrs Thin Man and was voted 'Queen of Hollywood' in the Thirties for her dazzling period of success in sharp and sweet comedies; Jean Peters was a star from her first film to her bowing out to become the second Mrs Howard Hughes, playing a succession of untamed minxes, Indians, Mexicans and spitfire pirates; Elaine Stewart specialized in Arab princesses; Jeanne Crain, Ava Gardner, Jennifer Jones and Susan Kohner played Negroes; Marilyn Watts became Mara Corday (all the better to cast you as Fifties spitfires, my dear!); Rita Gam played silent and sexy Indians; Peggy Middleton from Vancouver messed around on the fringe of film for years until her name was changed to Yvonne de Carlo and her face was covered with a yashmak; the French girl Yvonne Furneaux's black hair and long eyes qualified her for slave queens of Babylon – epics were big in the declining Fifties; you could take a little money and a little actress and go to some poor wretched parched country and get a lot of effect (landscape, cheap labour, native extras) for a little money. On the other hand – holding the other dye – Ida Lupino played WASPy Thirties ingénues; Concetta Ingolia became the brittle blonde Connie Stevens in Fifties gook like *Eighteen And Anxious* and *Young And Dangerous*. Even Rita Hayworth, *the* redhead, was dyed down from being Margarita Cansino. She gave the redhead the glitter of the blonde with the depth of the brunette.

What does it say about racial purity that the best blondes have all been brunettes (Harlow, Monroe, Bardot)? I think it says that we are not as white as we think. I think it says that Pure is a Bore.

Chapter Seven
HOMOSEXUALS' GIRLS

Feminine homosexual men, *queens* if you must, exist in inverse ratio amongst a country's homosexual population to their existence in that country's minds and nightmares. Around eighty per cent of homosexuals, masculinist homosexuals – the old, married, pictures-in-the-wallet, lost-weekend kind and the new, neurotic, moustachioed macho type – have masses in common with heterosexual men: they despise women, they are happiest with their own sex and so on. When they go to the movies they probably choose to see a war-as-spectacle Coppola or Scorsese or Cimino film – men in close and sweaty contact with men, yards of khaki and not a woman in sight.

But it is the despised and dying breed of queens who make a big splash, who influence styles and stand out a mile, visible and vulnerable and much braver than the over-compensating Ultramen could ever hope to be, even dressed in their hardest leather. It is they who are interesting – and their tender, living love for a dead Hollywood is riveting.

Which film stars do queens *not* like? The boyish and the Latin and the beatnik beauty – no Hepburns or Lorens or Bardots for them. These categories smack too much of carelessness, of beauty without trying. I have a friend who by day drives a cab and looks like a Marlboro Man but at night is the second best Jean Harlow I have ever seen. He summed up the kind of film star he adores, brutally and brilliantly, when he said, 'I like actresses who look as if they've spent five hours putting themselves together – and even *then* they don't look right.'

Most out-and-out sex goddesses were too authentically beautiful and desirable to men to appeal to the homosexual, to whom men are the target and women the decoy. One reason why homosexuals dislike women is that they have to compete with women to get men – 'If there were no women, *we'd* be the only girls in the world,' said my friend dreamily. 'Just like in jail.'

Marilyn is tolerated and even wept over when a queen is tipsy – 'but I don't think I'd like her if she was alive. She was artificial, okay, but she put it together too well. No man could ever look like that. I like her now, and my friends do – but to be a perfectly truthful bitch about it, I'd have to say that any dead film star is a good film star as far as we're concerned.'

The only sex symbol to amass a camp following whilst still alive was Jayne Mansfield – one of her closest friends was a queen who claims that he was responsible for teaching her everything she knew about appreciating male behinds: 'We were almost married. We *should* have married.' Mansfield mocked herself and heterosexual sex, especially when she realized that America did not regard her as that gorgeous piece any more – Julie Christie and a certain French *bébé* had swung into sex-dreams by then – and relegated her from the big screen to the cabaret trashcans. Her life was one long bust-up – always too drunk to walk onto a plane or a stage, always a divorce, a dead end, a decapitation. She was born with two big advantages in the game of being a woman and she still made a mess of things. She's a comfort to queens in that they can look at her and gloat '*I* could do better than that.'

If Jayne Mansfield represents all that queens despise about women, Marlene Dietrich is the apex of their aspirations. 'She walks and talks and looks

MM: the laugh was on her

Marlene Dietrich: more man than you'll ever be, more woman than you'll ever get

like the most successful TV *ever*,' said my friend. 'You must put this in your book – that American psychic or something who predicted in the Seventies that Mae and Marlene and Garbo would die in the Eighties and one of them would prove to be a man. Well, Mae's gone and Greta's going to live for ever – you know who *I* think is the lucky boy.'

'She has children,' I told him.

'So? Maybe she's their father.'

They idolize Dietrich. They admire Mae West, for the way she was always *conscious* of the homosexual audience (as early as 1927 she wrote and appeared in a stage play called *The Drag* – 'I knew all these gay chorus-boys – what chorus-boy isn't? – they made hats for my mother, they were real fun'), for the way she attracted and talked to men the way they wished *they* could (in *Myra Breckinridge*, 1970, to a roomful of eager young men: 'I'm a little tired tonight – one of you boys will have to go home'), for the gutsy and gracious way she grew old – 'Time will turn you into a hag if you don't show the bitch who's boss.'

They bleed for the tortured tradition of the tormented trouper as personified by Judy Garland, make-up put on with a trowel and a shaky hand, combining the queen's wildest dreams of exhibitionism with their worst suspicions about the stability of the opposite sex. In the early Sixties, Maria Callas was a common camp taste 'because she's killing her voice, not

Mae West in a dress that would look better on a chorus boy

holding anything back for retirement' as one fey fan put it.

But the star they have always *identified* with is Joan Crawford, whose career declined into the doldrums *three times*; three times she came back more powerful than before. She was a clawer; she re-created herself, as feminine homosexuals dream of doing until the day they die or have the Operation. From a poor and ugly childhood through several changes of name and husband – all in a mad search for elusive CLASS, which queens ache for totally, finding it next to impossible to tone themselves down or be subtle – through an operation to have her back teeth removed – all the better to see your cheekbones, my dear! – it all adds up to the longest film career ever recorded – 1925 to 1975. Crawford often appeared unintentionally ridiculous in her mid-period Forties films as a suburban Boadicea, and the domestic hells in which she finds herself, the vicious daughters and vile husbands, make out an argument against the heterosexual marriage and the nuclear family that the most evangelical camp crusader would find it hard to outdo. She was liked for her exaggeration of herself – her bow-tie mouth, her padded shoulders, her staring eyes, her bandbox sterility – at the height of her domestic agonies there is never a beauty spot out of place. This may be why *Whatever Happened To Baby Jane?*, which found Crawford and her *bête noire* Bette Davis circling each other in a sadistic minuet and both looking like trash, was such a wow with queens then and has been ever since.

'Oh, come *on* now!' sniggered my friend. 'You're going to make out we only go for Miss Crawford because she was some kind of comedy turn! Just because we laugh at her doesn't mean we don't love the old bitch. You laugh at *any* of your friends if they flounce it up too much – it doesn't mean anything *hostile*. What Joan Crawford – and most of all Bette Davis – is to me is *relief*, a way to *relax* – I know relaxation is the last thing you associate with either of them, but listen: when I watch them I feel as though I'm in a country where we're all speaking the same language at last. I don't feel as if I'm the wrong sex, but I do feel I'm in a strait-jacket; I'm looking like *this*, like a hunk, I'm stuck in that car, men are talking to me about football, girls are crossing their legs and showing their stocking tops in the mirror and giving me the glad eye and *I couldn't care less*. I can't speak that language. I'm like an actor with no script and I've been ad-libbing the same scene for two years now! I'm shut up in some strong and silent shoebox – and can you imagine how good it makes me feel when I see Joan Crawford making a Command Performance out of lighting a cigarette? It *looks* like comedy to *you* – but a girl can *act* like Joan Crawford does and at worst she'll be accused of being a melodramatic bitch or a show-off. I can go home and get out the video and watch *Mildred Pierce* and put on a good dress and I don't need anything more. That's my food, my sleep, my shoulder to cry on. Did you ever hear of anyone who hated their life-support machine? You may have a flaming faggot's taste in movies, kid, but your perspective is pure Puritan. And your opinion of what we really feel about the people we say we worship – we're not a pack of coyotes, you know.'

Nevertheless, self-parody and over-emphatic emoting always draws the coyote vote at the box-office. Faye Dunaway immersed herself in the persona of Joan Crawford in preparation for playing her in the disastrous *Mommie Dearest*. What was meant to be a serious and searing film did the rounds as a farce after primarily homosexual American audiences took to brandishing wire coat-hangers in imitation of a key scene. A friend of my friend even took a small but real *axe* to the cinema and waved it to roars of encouragement when Miss Dunaway bawled 'Christina, bring the axe!'

When Tallulah Bankhead opened in 1956 as Blanche DuBois she attracted an audience that was ninety-five per cent homosexual. They came because they had heard that Bankhead's performance would be a 'hoot'; they laughed incessantly and the actress, for whom the play was something of a last chance to be reckoned with, left the stage distraught. Her secretary brilliantly defined her heartbreaking appeal for the audience she was saddled with: 'She was doing onstage what they all did when they played dress-ups with their friends. Here was *their* kind of talk, *their* gestures.' They liked her because they were travesties of film stars and so, by this late stage in her career, was she.

Joan Crawford: beauty with cruelty

It was after Bankhead's Blanche that word went around the homosexual grapevine that Tennessee Williams had actually *created* the character as a drag queen – *that's* why she won't let Mitch get too close, not simply wrinkles. This wishful thinking was the latest in a long line of insolent invert interpretations of Williams' work, determined as American homosexuals were to make him *their* playwright.

He is too good and his plays are on too grand a scale to be stuck up some gay ghetto and forgotten. His main preoccupation is not the violence between men in torn T-shirts and fading females but the SOUTH. His loathing of his home is often and wilfully read as a loathing of women – but his women are pathetic because of their heritage, not their sex. They are sick not with some sex-related complaint, but with the sickness of the South – they are carriers, as the powerless Southern Belle came to be idealized and rationalized as a symbol in need of protection from black freedom and Northern normality. They are the secret side of Scarlett O'Hara, the never-ending scream that skulks behind the simper.

When Hollywood as she is *really* spoken died in the Fifties, it was inevitable that some brave queen would try to *be* his dead idol, to follow in her stiletto footsteps, to keep the faith, frivolous as that faith may seem to anyone who never cried at a movie. As they might have once run to the Sign, they ran to Andy Warhol. There are more theories about Andy Warhol than there are seconds in a century, so let me just explain him in a

Tallulah Bankhead doing what she was best at – smoking a cigarette

Andy Warhol: the boy who would be a brand name

few words that will mean as much to the naïve as to the knowledgeable. As a child of immigrants, his ambition was to be an All-American BRAND NAME – as big as the Hollywood Sign, for instance. He wanted to make films and the queens wanted to be stars; what they had in common was that *they wanted Hollywood back*, more than Warhol would ever admit to himself.

Although his films are the antithesis of big budget Technicolor, they are so through lack of funding and not intention. The clues are barely hidden and easily collected; at one time he talked of changing the Factory's name to, simply, HOLLYWOOD; one of Carmen Miranda's shoes is enshrined above his fireplace; his films were as likely as not called *Lana Turner, Lupe, Batman, Dracula, Hedy, Tarzan And Jane Regained, Salome And Delilah*; he went out of his way to become an intimate of Paulette Goddard; in 1965 he finally made several trips to his Mecca and came back each time decrying its *naturalness* — its death. His much-vaunted 'emptiness', his efforts to 'love' his tape recorder and his TV is nothing more than a hangover from Hollywood — the immigrant child's sulk and depression that glamour, the thing he was raised on and the only thing that America did best, is gone before he ever had a chance to touch it. In the 'underground' (so called, I suppose, because watching them is about as much fun as riding a subway in the rush-hour) films of other countries, Hollywood's existence is never hinted at; American underground is a strangled gasp from a ghost's last grasp.

His early films starred dizzy, druggy girls — most strikingly the harlot-Hepburn, Edie Sedgwick — but they were really only pale, messed up shadows of the Chelsea Girl. What he wanted was Hollywood, so what he wanted was drag queens; 'Drags are ambulatory archives of ideal movie-star womanhood.' He found Mario Montez, a civil servant who had attempted (somewhat pitifully) to model himself on the lines of the Cobra Woman herself — he dressed up only for the screen and lived in fear that his friends and family would find him out. Every night he prayed for his parents and all the dead film stars he loved — Linda Darnell, James Dean, Dorothy Dandridge. Candy Darling was Warhol's favourite queen — she was Everyblonde, with a Kim Novak voice, clothed in Ann Sheridan sundresses and satin and tat, tall and spectacular with no teeth of her own. Her real name was Jimmy Slattery. Her friend Jackie Curtis wrote plays with great titles — *Glamour, Glory And Gold* was one — and wore bushy hennaed hair and Forties dresses fastened with brooches; Jackie and Candy lived together, resembling the Misfits Isabel and Roslyn.

These queens, especially Candy Darling, ached for Hollywood. Warhol's dinky hand-held camera, the art house regulars that passed for an audi-ence, the grainy black and white of the film — how could it compare? Warhol's movies were home movies, and home movies are not interesting unless your friends are in them. Also, home movies could not be further removed from HOLLYWOOD. Warhol the user of popular myth was prob-ably *used* more often than not by bad actors who saw him as nothing more Machiavellian than a stepping stone to the real screen. But not one Warhol star (*Superstar* — some hope!) was ever snapped up by the New Hollywood, not even real beauties like Jane Forth and Joe Dallesandro. Baby Jane Holzer was considered for *Candy*, but eventually snubbed for the raw and sweet young Swede Ewa Aulin.

Andy Warhol said, 'The people I loved were the leftovers of show-business, turned down at auditions all over town. They couldn't do some-thing more than once, but their once was better than anyone else's.' Candy Darling lived the line. When the news that *Myra Breckenridge* was to be made into a movie appeared in the trade papers, Candy wrote to everyone involved telling them that she WAS Myra. When Raquel Welch was named as the sex-change star, Darling wrote begging letters, begging everyone to please, please reconsider. There was no reply and Candy Darling lost heart and hope. All her life she had been rejected but she had survived by holding on to the belief that Hollywood would always take her in, consecrating her life as she had to keeping the dream alive. But what did the Hollywood Sign know of Andy Warhol?

Or Candy Darling as she staggered on her high heels through her half-life. Tennessee Williams starred her in *Small Craft Warnings*, but even that was off-Broadway. In 1974 she contracted cancer and lay dying for weeks before receiving treatment fit for a film star – a funeral uptown at Frank Campbell's.

Deceased Deutsche director Rainer Werner Fassbinder would have app-reciated such a send-off, but it is doubtful whether the earnest German types and bimbo boys with whom he surrounded himself would appreciate such a frivolous film-buff fantasy. R.W. started out as your average underground groundhog, just teasing himself every now and then (à la La Warhola) with a hot hint of that homosexuals' heaven, Hollywood. Towards the end of his life, as if sensing that it was his last exit to Glamour Gulch, R.W. plunged straight into the deep end of that heart-shaped swimming-pool of tears and eternal triangles to make his stocking tops and swastikas schlock for the rest of his days.

Celluloid homosexuality *in flagrante delicto* has always been a boring business. Lovely actresses have been used in lousy films as lesbians to titil-late tut-tutting men – Jean Seberg as *Lilith*, Candice Bergen as Lakey in *The Group*, Stephan Audran and Jacqueline Sassard as *Les Biches*, Mariel Hemingway in *Personal Best*. In *Making Love*, Kate Jackson is married to a tootsie who selfishly turns queer on her and tries to set up house with Ursula Andress's flighty boyfriend. As if they had already realized that their own film is a stinker, the participants sit around watching vintage froth such as *Raintree County* and *Cat On A Hot Tin Roof*, often quoting whole passages verbatim. 'Oh God!' said my friend, 'You're *not* writing about that drear...why don't you tell them about the last great camp gesture ever put on film?' Which is? – 'That nightmarish Uncle Tom ballet from *The King And I* – 1958.' It was 1956 actually, but proceed. 'I love it because it has kitsch, confusion, comedy, cruelty and a sacrifice scene at the end to cry at!'

He is right – but, poor dear, he is also the last in his line, I fear. The way the cinema is going – inward, inward, forever inward – there is precious little future for his half-breed. The day will not come when the boy is born who wants to look like Meryl Streep.

Chapter Eight
JAMES BOND GIRLS

Britain is a nation of spies.

We excel at it. Our public schools are institutes of espionage – little rich waifs in cold imperial nurseries; see them run to Mother Russia!

After the War, Britain let itself be led into the American fold – the American stranglehold. We were too tired to argue. But we yearned towards Russia all the same, all the time. Like them we were invaded, by bombs if not by butchers; the fighting working class and the skiving Intelligence élite felt that Britain should have adopted an avenging Russian attitude to humbled Nazi Germany rather than go along with the American view of justice – 'Hey, Fritz – you're okay!' The working class showed their sympathies by ousting Churchill and voting in a Labour government and even a handful of Communist MPs. The skiving élite proved theirs by spying.

Guy Burgess, the brilliant and bitchy bender! Donald Maclean, the quiet collator of crucial facts – 'My God, he knows everything!' an American Security man blurted when he heard that Maclean had done a bunk! Anthony Blunt, a faithful servant and favourite of the Queen – and occasionally the USSR! Alan Nunn May, protégé of Einstein, who felt it was only fair play that the Russians should have the Bomb too – he even sent them a sample of uranium! Lonsdale, Blake, even foreigners like Fuchs and Pontecorvo, knew that Britain was the best base from which to conduct a long-distance love affair with a certain Soviet Union. But every time we come back to the Spy of Spies, liar of liars, Kim Philby.

The most successful spy ever to have lived, Philby worked for Russia from 1934 to 1963 as well as being head of the special department of M16 created with the express purpose of monitoring Russian Intelligence. When he reached Moscow his debriefing took *two years*. The completion in 1965 was celebrated by the awarding of the Soviet Union's 'Red Banner

of Honour', one of the highest orders that can be bestowed for services to the country. Philby was made a Colonel in the KGB – in 1978 he was promoted to General. Philby the Faithful...Philby the Philanderer! His steely dedication in his secret life contrasted stunningly with the sleaziness of his private life. He loved to drink, and would drink anything. He once returned from a hostess's bathroom smacking his lips and exclaiming, 'What's that splendid stuff you've got in there?' – it was eau de cologne. He went for girls in a big way – English Fascists, Austrian-Jewish Communists, American nothings and, of course, Russian girls – and could have given Zsa Zsa a run for her money when it came to the saunter to the altar.

In a world of nine to five and compromise and the revision of dreams, Philby is a singularly glamorous creature. He lived the life that popular songs are made of, He Did It All For Love. Forbidden love! Secret love! Long lost love – at long last love! He was simply *the best* at what he chose to do and thus made fawning fans out of magnificent minds. We *are* a nation of spies, or our greatest writers – John Le Carré and Graham Greene – would not chart their progress so constantly. Both have written Forewords to Philby books (an industry in themselves); both veer from adoring to admonishing and back again, helplessly. Philby the Pink is their ink; when they try to make up a spy, a certain smile or a sentimentality or a sneer of *his* runs onto the page and thereon runs the show.

The Spy Nation's cinema-goers were soon ripe and ready for a celluloid spy of their own – tough, cool, sexy and decidedly apolitical. Commitment to a Cause would entail monologues and motivation and character-development, which would waste valuable kissing and killing time. He could have been Anyhunk, so prepared to adore him were the Spy Nation's audience, but he happened to be James Bond – coy and brutal creation of Ian Fleming's as celebrated in a dozen or so books.

Bond was sold as a spy to a nation of spies and to a Westworld hungry for even more proof that we were a nation of spies, but he really spied only once in a true blue moon. His real business is killing – his code-name 007, he explains patiently in the first film, *Dr No*, means he has a License to Kill – and we all know that spies are too clever to kill.

Bond kills with neither emotion nor enjoyment and approaches girls in the same way. The only things he seems to find pleasure in are his famous gadgets, which he plays with so incessantly that you'd think he'd go blind in the first reel. Most of the plots revolve around Bond trying to save the world from a mad Machiavellian scientist (usually effeminate, this being indicated by much wearing of rings and stroking of cats) – a sketchy and stretchy kind of storyline which the audience can automatically take in, disregard and then pay attention to the serious business of spotting the new gadgets...and the new girls.

In the mid-Sixties, to be chosen as a James Bond Girl became the high-

Left
Falling in love again: Ian Fleming contemplates his umpteenth Bond book

Below left
Ursula, undressed to kill

Below
Pussy Galore: butch goddess of *Goldfinger*

sex-status equivalent of being a pre-War Vargas Girl or Ziegfield Girl. In the decade of the unimpeachable Chelsea Girl, Bond Girls were odd creatures – a hybrid of a mannequin and a museum piece.

Because Ian Fleming was ancient and had no idea how modern girls behaved, the antiquity of the sex-banter sits strangely amongst the futuristic gadgets and fab gear; Bond will raise an eyebrow, Bond Girl will wiggle and giggle and that's how they get their kicks – that's your lot! Being a Bond Girl soon looked like nothing more than a one-way ticket to obscurity. The only girls who got remembered were girls who had something gigantic or gimmicky about them. Ursula Andress, slinking out of the sea in a bikini and a Bowie knife! The first Bond Girl and the most unforgettable – although the bikini, thought to be so daring at the time, rather resembles a chuddah compared to the tangas of today. Like Jean Shrimpton's two-inches-above-the-knee dress that caused shrieks at the Australian races, it's hard to see what the fuss was about.

Of course, I am being naive. What all the fuss was about was Ursula Andress, *looking like that* – a big Sex Doll body with a European matinée idol's face walking out of the sea and into the Sixties – *some sort of epic evolution*.

She was perfect as Honey Ryder, almost as perfect as Sean Connery's James Bond. Just as Marilyn could make the sickening Sex Doll lovable when she wrapped her soul around it, so could Connery, a working-class Scot, save and launch the effete Fleming hero by being himself and not the pompous, public-schooled Pimpernel of Fleming's prolific fantasies. Andress and Connery had lots in common – they were both beautiful on the grand scale, they had been making films for a long time to no effect (Andress for eight years since she was eighteen, Connery for eight years since he was twenty-four) and they both ruined their roles for future impostors by making such staggeringly swashbuckling impressions on a person.

Right enough, the Bond Girl of *From Russia With Love* (1963) evaporated like vapid vapour after Andress. The female who stole the show was the Bond Brute – Rosa Klebb as played by Lotte Lenya and her amazing stiletto-*toed* shoes. Fleming's ongoing mucky interest in lesbians can be seen in the way *Goldfinger* (1964) featured Honor Blackman as Pussy Galore, a sexy Sapphic in leather. Whereas Klebb is an ugly lesbian and as such wants only to brawl, Galore is gorgeous and so, after a few preliminary scratches (and judo throws – she was *The Avengers'* Kathy Gale, remember), gives in and purrs like a good Pussy.

Goldfinger is an exception re the Bond roster because it is rash with its female gimmicks, using three in one film instead of saving two for a pallid plot on a rainy day. As well as Pussy Pervert, *Goldfinger* is remembered for Shirley Eaton as Jill Masterton lying on a red couch oozing gold paint from every pore. Then there are the fighting gypsies Bond encounters and the camera masturbates over up in the hills – the catfight, always a big favourite with little men who want to feel big. Even civilized, civil men appreciate a catfight – you can see a girl getting slapped around without doing it yourself and feeling like a bully or watching a screen man doing it and condoning brutality.

Such a vivid harem of fantasies – a queer girl in leather, a dead girl in gold, a pair of pretty pugilists in a pear tree – used up so quickly inevitably drained the next films of flak and fun. In *Thunderball* Claudine Auger is a pretty little nothing while *You Only Live Twice* is a sentimental oriental blur. For some odd slip of contract or other, *Casino Royale* belonged to another company and in 1967 it was filmed with David Niven and became an instant *objet d'art*. The slick set had been saying for ages that the Bond films were gems of conscious camp but really the only comedy came in when Connery was required to speak an irredeemably ridiculous lecher-line to a girl; to spare his blushes he would raise his raven eyebrows and insinuate the asinine line à la Mae.

David Niven knew how old the young girls around him – Jackie Bisset, Angela Scoular, very Chelsea – made him look and so he delivered his lines like a patrician pantomimer, tongue Superglued in his cheek, whereas Connery's was always too busy in the ear of some girl. Ursula Andress reappears by vox-popular demand, but she appears baffled and has not packed her bikini.

Perhaps the films would have picked up a little if she had. Because by 1971 James Bond has had his day and his decade. The American audience has always been gigantic and grateful for any crumbs from Bond's break-fast tray so the next film was set in the American hamlet of Las Vegas and co-starred the American actress Jill St John. Connery was cuter than ever but *Diamonds Are Forever* was his last Bond film – or so he said.

In 1972 the new Bond, George Lazenby, is unveiled in *On Her Majesty's Secret Service*. Diana Rigg, a thoughtful actress, plays Tracy, the girl Bond marries only for her to be shot dead by dastardly bastards as they drive off into the sunset. Lazenby puts in a strong and sweet performance obviously modelled – to his credit – on Connery's, but there is a skeleton in his closet. Or rather, a chocolate bar in his scrapbook.

As a starving actor, George made a TV commercial touting a bar called Big Fry. He staggered into town carrying the huge sweetmeat across his considerable shoulders. When he appeared on the big Bond screen people tended not to melt with sheer molten awe but to shout 'BIG FRY!' as a friendly greeting.

The financial investment in a Bond film is formidable – scenery, stunts, a cast of thousands of pretty girls and petty criminals – and Bond is the pivot who must be one hundred per cent believable if he hopes to carry off this

On Her Majesty's Secret Service: small fry meets Shakespearian Bond girl

stupid fantasy. Outside of the Sixties charmed circle it is suddenly obvious that the films *are* stupid, as stupid and over-compensatingly masculine as a chest wig. Big 'George' Fry, likeable as he was, was tainted with tackiness and touting; Caesar's secret agent must be above reproach, and Lazenby laid him open to being a figure of fun. He was banished to the land of television tooth-rot for ever.

Roger Moore had been making films since 1945 and had proved spectacularly unsuccessful on the big screen. In the Sixties he applied his small talent to the small screen and found slight success as *The Saint*, a dapper detective and perfect gentleman created by one Leslie Charteris – an alias of a Singapore man with a name like Hoo Flung Dung and a kind colonial kid's ideal of the English hero. Moore was a natural; *he* was *his* ideal of a perfect English gentleman although just as far removed from the actuality as Mr Charteris. *Classy* became more and more confused with *shallow* in Moore's mind until his acting was literally unbearable to watch. You could blush until you were a Belisha beacon and die a thousand spiritual deaths on his behalf but he still wouldn't stop using self-satisfied smirks as full stops or talking to girls as though they were bolshy budgies; and when Moore wanted to express surprise – this is the classic – he invariably looked as though someone was giving him a sudden enema. Naturally, he jumped on James Bond like a duck on dough-boys! Class at last! Big screen! Technicolor! He was forty-six and greedy. In 1973 he made *Live And Let Die*, Jayne

Jayne Seymour: playing Solitaire

Maud Adams: always a Bond girl, never a star

Seymour playing Solitaire. Moore's mega-narcissism was contagious; not one response was ever wrung out of a Bond Girl from this point on.

Sean Connery could always talk up something warm with his Bond Girl; Moore inspected his playmates as if they were privates on parade. To give him his due he was much truer to the awful authentic printed word: Fleming's hero is forever fussing over the details of his diet and the form of the food on his plate – the taste is never mentioned. Once Connery quit it was the same with the Bond Girls; the substance of sex is less than zero – the showing is all.

In 1974 there was *The Man With The Golden Gun* – Britt Ekland doing her well-known showroom-dummy routine and Maud Adams, the dark and Garboesque Swedish cover girl, making her debut into a career of celluloid negligence. 1977's *The Spy Who Love ↲ Me* revived the flagging fortunes of the Bond empire by casting Barbara Bach as a Red Army General – reintroducing the carnal conflict between conqueror and Communist girl was a much-needed novelty that made a change from the puny and predictable pushovers that Bond had gotten used to pushing over. There was dynamism and at long last a new deviation in their dalliance – when the capitalist conqueror sexually subdues the Communist girl he can feel for a few hours that he has achieved that most impossible of all deadend daydreams: halting the historical Communist harvesting of the World. A thrill worthy of any *ubermensch*.

Lois Chiles was a beautiful but lost cause in *Moonraker* and 1981's *For*

Your Eyes Only whisked Carole Bouquet from Buñuel to banal. *Octopussy*'s only highspot was the return of the magnificent Maud Adams in the title role.

But hers was not the only comeback into the land of the licensed to kill. In 1984 *Never Say Never Again* appeared, with Kim Basinger as Good Blonde, Barbara Carrera as Wicked Brunette – and Sean Connery as James Bond (an ironic title, it might as well have been called *Never Say You'll Never Make Another James Bond Film Again*). Well into his fifties, the thrill was indubitably gone – and so, sadly, was a great deal of Mr Connery's hair. In America alone the film lost six million dollars – took six million dollars less at the box-office than it cost to make. For the first time in his long cinematic career, James Bond was on the road to that most unvirile of resting-places – the art-house, white elephants' graveyard of the poor, non-profit-making film.

1985 saw the official, most recent Bond film, *A View To A Kill*, with fifty-eight-year-old Roger Moore (the only film actor currently labouring under a name as pornographically pun-ridden as Rock or Power) protecting pretty Tanya Roberts, the blonde furniture mandatory in modern Bond films. The real female focus is Grace Jones, in whom the girl and gadget become one in a way they have not since Rosa Klebb's stiletto toes; as May Day, her body itself is a deadly weapon rather than a place for Bond to make the usual safe deposit. When they screw, she even GETS ON TOP. Ian Fleming must have turned in his urn.

More than twenty years after his first big screen bang, both Bonds were approaching pensionable age – licensed to ride a bus free of charge! The girls remained twenty-six while the Bonds became sixty, literally old enough to be their grandfathers – and the film critics were ungallant enough to mention it to a man. At this moment, Chubby Zucchini and his merry casting agents are looking for a boy to do a man's job. But need they bother? Ian Fleming claimed, from the depths of his own private sexual maelstrom, that he wrote his books for 'warm-blooded heterosexuals', but surely only cold-blooded homosexuals could derive entertainment from spectacles which show heterosexuality as such a boring business when practised with good girls, and such a treacherous one when practised with bad girls.

Bond should be given a decent burial. Like a torn paper dress or a pink Dynel wig, it took the cold kinkiness of the Sixties to suspend cred where he was concerned. Among the jolly ghostbusters, butch Indiana Joneses and conscripted Rambos, Bond's casual, aristocratic approach to the nitty-gritty business of killing seems indecently snobbish and effete. Now must be the time for him to marry the matronly Moneypenny, get a desk job and trade in his License for a library ticket. Old spies never die – they just get debriefed...

Chapter Nine
YOUNG GIRLS

All desirable actresses are by definition young; but beyond the Gamine and the Spitfire, beyond the Chelsea Girl and the Sex Doll who are incidentally young there is the girl whose chief selling point is her youth.

Very smooth, young girls, no stretch marks on their minds, eyes that have seen too little and drunk too few bullshots to be bloodshot. And for the man who can't quite measure up, there's no track record or score card...

As there are two kinds of women, so there are two kinds of young girl. The man who goes to see Aileen Quinn as *Annie* with sex on his mind is immediately a pervert, but if he watches Pia Zadora play the fifteen-year-old Kady in *Butterfly* without a *frisson* his normality may be called into question to an even greater degree. The justification for feeling lust in the second instance could be of course that Miss Zadora is a married woman in her twenties *pretending* to be jailbait, and that is the safety valve. But then one thinks of the beautiful Brooke Shields, who was sold as a fully-fashioned, grown-up sex-child at the age of twelve in Louis Malle's soft-focus surf through prostitution, *Pretty Baby*, and the flip-side of that film with its sepia-tinted, lazy Southlands titillation, the nightmarish and indisputably factual (just walk down the streets of your capital city...) *Taxi Driver*, with Jodie Foster's twelve-year-old pretty baby buried alive amongst the city's ugly adults. Chronologically, Miss Shields and Miss Foster were children at the time of these performances, yet they had forfeited their right to be respected à la Little Orphan. By indulging in sex they have given up the right to be treated with the chaste chivalry that is the prerogative of the girl-child, and must from now on be judged as grown women are, not by their intelligence or their goodness but by their physical availability.

As Europe is thought to be the home of the older woman who teaches

Pia Zadora: from rags to Riklis

Brooke Shields in *Pretty Baby*, star of the school for Malle-adjusted children

Jodie hustles; Hinckley's fists clench in the cheap seats

the acne-ridden adolescent boy a thing or two (note the Latinate callousness of Anne Bancroft – née Anna Maria Italiano – as the most famous of the American copies, Mrs Robinson), America is the home of the young girl. American women themselves are painfully (literally painfully, in the case of the mandatory cosmetic surgery that has ravished all of the female population over forty) aware of this, and American film stars obligingly kill themselves or destroy themselves slowly with drink or drugs or divorce when the wrinkles start to show. The young girl is an American institution, and in her country's attitude to her one of Freud's most tired old dictums springs vividly to life – 'Where there is love there is no desire; where there is desire there is no love.'

The first generation of film stars were very young, in their middle teens – Mabel Normand, Mae Marsh, Colleen Moore and, of course, Mary Pickford, who played little girls until she had turned thirty – and the pantomime vamps of the time were needed purely as foils to their chastity and not really as attractions in themselves. The Thirties was a prime time for children of the beloved kind, because the Thirties was America's first terrible decade of reckoning-up – what it had taken out of the world so far, and what the world was about to make it pay for, first by the Depression and then by the War – and the child, innocent and unbattered, was a sentimental refuge and relief, a Statuette of Liberty in whose simple-minded

Colleen Moore: angelic adolescent, seen and not heard

optimism one could bask for a few hours in the darkness. One could cry at the Orphan's progress through the big wide world, and pretend that that was all one was crying about.

Ignorance was bliss in those days when there was so much wickedness consuming Europe – and ignorance was box-office. Deanna Durbin from the age of fifteen kept Universal afloat single-handedly with her soprano voice and her sumptuous figure. At the end of her teens, she was given the Special Oscar which is usually given to old hands on their deathbeds and to child actors on their equivalent, the dreaded twentieth birthday. Also popular in the Thirties were Peggy-Ann Garner, Diana Lynn, Gloria Jean, Bonita Granville and Jane Withers – pre-teens and teenagers with soft centres and sharp tongues; all decidedly unsexy and all thought up because the sweetness-and-light market had been cornered by a mere six-year-old before the Thirties were halfway through.

She was, of course, Shirley Temple, at once the singular and the archetypal child star as Marilyn Monroe is the sex symbol. Temple made her first film at the age of four, and two years later appeared indisputably above the title on the credits. Her timing, reaction and sly wit made her the top American star from 1935 to 1938 and helped her replace her antithesis, Greta Garbo, as the top star of the Thirties. After the initial introspection of the Depression, when America had morbidly enjoyed moping along with Garbo, the nation realized that it had to look on the bright side – and

Deanna Durbin: her pure soprano could shatter the arms of CBS announcers at a hundred paces

Shirley Temple: sugar and steel

126

Elizabeth Taylor: she'd wait at home for Lassie -- but not for Nicky, Eddie or Ricky

nothing could have been brighter than Shirley Temple.

She was the ultimate expression of a sexless adoration of the young girl, and at the time the purity of the passion was never called into question. Since then frivolous cynics have smirked about her appeal to old men, and in *Myra Breckinridge* the bored-beyond-belief Myra watches the clip from *Heidi* in which Temple, attempting to milk a goat, gets squirted in the face, in an attempt to become aroused. I personally think that America's worship at the temple of Shirley was above reproach, and that the hip sniggers are little eruptions of envy from a culture that wears sex like a monkey on the back and longs to be free of worldliness for a weekend. But there is no denying that America turned away from Shirley Temple as she showed signs of that rare deviation, adolescence, like a Big Daddy who cannot stand to see his little girl growing up. Child stars rarely become adult stars — there are exceptions such as Elizabeth Taylor and Natalie Wood who went from cute childhood through pretty teenage into beautiful maturity that was simply too scarce to be allowed to get away, and Judy Garland, who swept through her career on one long surge of nervous energy and incessant sobbing as she tugged on the public's heartstrings. When pre-picture publicity trumpets HER FIRST KISS! you just know that it will also be one of her last big hits. Her value is that, in a world of sex, she *doesn't* get kissed.

Natalie Wood: cute childhood

Judy Garland: a star is torn

Hayley Mills: pre-puberty and rites of menace in *Tiger Bay*

One young girl who served this function in the Forties was Margaret O'Brien, a cute and clever actress who made her first film at four and received an Oscar at seven in 1944. Her performance was always original and memorable, but she was suspended by MGM in 1950 for refusing to make *Alice In Wonderland* – showing the very spirit that made her so special. Her starring roles stopped after this, though she was a big hit as Beth, the sickly saint of *Little Women*, turning in a performance that could make a glass eye weep.

In the Fifties the swaggering, sexy goddess all but disappeared, and the female ideal became the Sex Doll, and the Sex Doll ideal was Marilyn – a little girl in all but vital statistics. For a while England took over the production of young girls, and they were good ones: Mandy Miller, the eight-year-old star of *Mandy*, who as a little deaf girl made the sickly Beth about as touchingly vulnerable as Hard-Hearted Hannah – she grew up to be ravishingly pretty and left films voluntarily; and Hayley Mills, who gave a swashbucklingly tomboyish performance at thirteen in *Tiger Bay*. Hollywood spotted Miss Mills, grew her blonde hair, washed her blonde skin and made her Disney's *Pollyanna*, for which she received an Oscar. Until 1966, when she was twenty, she played mischievous and chaste children. Back in Britain, her babyish prettiness meant that she ended up being menaced and seduced for a living and it was left to TV to make her a strong and subtle screen presence in the Eighties.

Had Hayley Mills not been British, and a member of a distinguished theatrical family, and remembered as Pollyanna and therefore a sacred stereotype, her looks would have picked her out as a nymphet supreme. In the late Fifties and early Sixties a new influx of girls appeared on the big screen and they were the first visible presence of the other kind of young girl, the girl who arouses sexually and is therefore bad. Her badness is given extra clout by the fact that she is *illegal*: if she is under eighteen a man can be ruined by falling victim to her vamping, he can lose everything. She is bad yet the law is on her side; she is a nymphet, and indicative of an age where youth is both worshipped and feared.

Post-War America was more affluent than ever, but unlike the period after the First World War, it did not feel particularly good about itself. Russia had fought harder and looked stronger. Communism, as a reaction to Fascism and the capitalism that had rocked the cradle, covered more than half the globe. The youth of America had an unspecific rage, and they fed it on the rock and roll that they had hijacked from the solace of the Negro – black music – and they re-created themselves as a persecuted minority.

Given a new minority, America blamed it for the current discontent; youth blamed their parents right back.

This did not grow into any kind of political confrontation – Rebel *Without* A Cause – but it did produce a kind of cultural apartheid. Kids wanted to be with kids, constantly. They wanted to get out of the houses where their parents were. One of the most popular rallying points was the drive-in, where you could be alone in your car while in close contact with your own kind. The success and death of James Dean in 1955 left the market open for anything in pedal-pushers that didn't want to go home, and the market became a swamp as the despised old men moved in to tout what the teenagers wanted.

In the late Fifties over half the population of America was under thirty – and half of those seemed to be appearing in films by American International Pictures, called AIP. AIP dealt in the light side of teenage separatism. Parents were not actively disliked in their films, they simply ceased to exist. The beach was recognized as another place where adults were not likely to be, and the Beach Party films were invented – my favourite title from the genre is *It's A Bikini World*. The beach films usually starred the beautiful Annette Funicello set against Frankie Avalon or Fabian, two singularly insipid pop singers of the day, and were dosed with a liberal helping of songs considered not fit for hard plastic – vinyl – but perfectly adequate for soft plastic – celluloid – seeing as all the teenage audience wanted was the ritual of the movie and were not interested or able to judge the quality of the merchandise. Besides, the more awful the band, the cheaper they could be hired, and these films were nothing if not money-hungry. In the decade of disastrous receipts at the box-office where the big studios were concerned, AIP raked it in. One classic of the genre, 1956's *Rock, Rock, Rock*, took *two weeks* to make; the budget would not have covered coffee on a legitimate studio effort.

These youth films did so well that many old movie stars, unable to find work with the ailing studios, put in hard labour on them – Buster Keaton, Barbara Stanwyck and Mickey Rooney were a few. They're still waiting for their Oscar nominations.

As the Sixties progressed and American society regressed, SURF crept out of the titles and RIOT and WILD moved ominously in – *Wild On The Beach*, *Wild In The Country* and *Wild In The Streets*; this last, made in 1968, was as far as youth-fear could go: a teenage rock star and a drug pusher get the age of majority lowered to fourteen and run for Presidential office on the ticket NEVER TRUST ANYONE OVER THIRTY. The teenage mindlessness so celebrated in the early films had mutated into malignance in a spurious attempt to be taken seriously. Mind you, this is not to suggest that the Beach Party films were not sincere and socially conscious movies. In 1963's *Horror Of Monster Beach*, an early ecologist gem, a skull on the seabed is affected by radiation, turns monster and heads for the beach in search of tasty teenage blood. Yeuuuch! But whatever the topic of the teen films, the girls were the important thing.

The AIP and associated films were a blessing to young actresses in the late Fifties; scarce screen work could be had for stripping down to nothing seedier than a bikini. Annette Funicello, Deborah Walley, Yvette Mimieux, Connie Stevens, Shelley Fabares – all constructed long careers in them. But others even moved into the mainstream from them – Paula Prentiss, the dark beauty and underrated comedienne, Carol Lynley and Tuesday Weld, both nymphets.

A young girl can only be a nymphet when she is looked at with the desirous eyes of an old man. The girls in bikinis dancing at beach parties do not look like anything exotic to the boys they dance with, but to old men they look like their own youth and dreams – that unattainable and that desirable. If you are going to aim at this delicate area, though, you must not make the mistake of making the appreciator of nymphets feel like a child molester – that universally reviled and repulsive reject. When Carroll Baker sucked her thumb at twenty-four in that big crib in the first frame of *Baby Doll* it was beyond a joke; Marilyn was going strong and sweet in that year, 1956, and the nation that loved her because she played the tot did not want their sickness shoved in their faces. The film was denounced from pulpits and a great proportion of the potential audience – respectable men with a yen for youngsters – probably stayed away for fear of being found out. Despite the sensational launch that the film gave her, Carroll Baker proved box-office poison and in her early thirties turned to softcore

Continental slop to keep her head above water.

In 1962 Sue Lyon played *Lolita*, and Stanley Kubrick showed craftiness in raising Lolita's age from twelve to fourteen. Censors stated that as Sue Lyon looked even older the film would be released without cuts. The result satisfied no one; the moralists screeched regardless, the lyricism of the book was lost and Miss Lyon did indeed seem so cool and autonomous that you would never have guessed the affair was taboo had the names been changed. Her career in films was similar to Carroll Baker's – a cross between casual and a casualty.

The trick was to slip nymphets into films by the back door and make them no younger than mid-teens. Physically they were recognizable: they were slight, with light hair and sweet faces and wistful manners, as though they were missing something – you, the father figure, of course!

A sort of Mecca of nymphets was the smalltown epic *Peyton Place*, written with a pen dipped in poison by Grace Metalious. In its long-running TV incarnation, the Metalious-role – author-outsider – of Allison was played by Mia Farrow, the thinking (and crooning) man's nymphet. Before that, though, were the films. Diane Varsi starred in the 1957 film and was being built into something big by her studio, Fox; but she was a sensitive girl who found the cinema not to her liking (Fox might have contributed to this, being notoriously shallow and callous where sensitive actresses were concerned) and before long ran away from her studio back to her home town, causing something of a sensation and causing the columnist Joe Hyams to trace her and quiz her about why she hated Hollywood. Hyams himself claims to have had something of a *satori* while talking to her concerning his own position in the ruins of Hollywood, but that's another (sob) story.

The next year *Return To Peyton Place* was made, Carol Lynley replacing Varsi in the central role. This movie elaborated on little orphan Allison's search for a man to fill the vacuum created by her unknown father, and also introduced the sad case of Selena Cross – the riveting Tuesday Weld – Allison's best friend who has been sexually abused by her stepfather since she was a child. It was a cinch for the nymphet appreciators in the audience; you could put yourself in the shoes of the daddy of your choice – good and gone or bad and bullying. Everyone else liked it too; even now made-for-TV *Peyton Place* films crop up occasionally, the name and legend intact but the cast tatty and totally changed.

Because *Peyton Place* and its spin-offs were emotional and successful, it was too easy to dismiss them as trivia; because Tuesday Weld, the best exponent of the nymphet, was beautiful and slick it was easy to dole out the same judgement to her. Hers has been one of the most chronically mismanaged careers of the post-War cinema, but she has been clever within the limits placed on her, and, unlike every other professional teenager of her era, she has stubbornly stayed on the big screen.

A showbusiness child, she was thirteen when she made the infamous *Rock, Rock, Rock* and a year older when Danny Kaye called her 'fourteen going on twenty-seven'. At seventeen she made *Sex Kittens Go To College*; at eighteen *Return To Peyton Place* and *Wild In The Country*. You would think her career was over here. But Tuesday Weld is interesting because, unlike all the other starlets who give it their best shot and retire hurt when stardom proper does not materialize, she has stayed around from the Fifties to the Eighties, never a household name, never unemployed and always looking not a day over seventeen.

In 1966 when she was twenty-three she played the industry idea of her own kind in *Lord Love A Duck* – the starstruck teenager who makes it from beach parties to big time. She was consciously becoming younger as she got older, a feat unique in a business where there is always a very good year of youth and beauty waiting to be brought up from the cellar and app-reciated. In 1968 she played the unhinged and homicidal Sue Ann in the brilliant and neglected *Pretty Poison*, making her co-star Tony Perkins look positively well-balanced. In 1970 at the age of twenty-seven she played the nasty nymphet in *I Walk The Line* and made Baby Doll and Lolita look just about ready to be put out to grass.

In recent years she has become a grown-up on screen (the dazed model

It's for you: the young Tuesday Weld hangs on for stardom

133

in *Play It As It Lays*, the beautiful older sister of Diane Keaton (what a joke!) in *Looking For Mr Goodbar*, the Vietnam veteran's shoulder to die on in *Dog Soldiers*) and even now shows no signs of becoming fashionable or credible. Still, she has given several great performances in several greatly underestimated films and will probably be unearthed and deified by some future film historian in the manner that Louise Brooks belatedly enjoys today. She perfected the Pia Zadora device of playing jailbait despite being a quarter of a century old – a sure way to cater to the lucrative lecher market without marking them out as molesters of infants – and will no doubt be around and beautiful long after Zadora's husband runs out of money to buy her a movie.

To be a constant nymph must be one of the hardest jobs around; think of Sandra Dee in 1959 at seventeen, the chaste and victimized heroine of *A Summer Place* as well as being *Gidget*. Sandra Dee was sort of the Uncle Tom of Teenage; one who wasn't snide or sarcastic or sex-mad or separatist, and Gidget was America's pat on the back, telling it it must be doing something right to produce a teenager as cute, high-spirited, decent and just all-round wonderful as Gidget (a grotesque abbreviation of girl-midget). Gidget was great box-office for a while – *Gidget Goes Hawaiian*(1961) and *Gidget Goes To Rome*(1963). There followed a huge gap as Dee went to seed in her mid-twenties to appear chubby and blowsy in *Gidget Grows Up*(1970) and finally did the only thing she was fit for by now – *Gidget Gets Married* (1972).

No matter how the young girl tried to cope with the fact that the early Sixties beach party had become the late Sixties wild party she seemed doomed. Sandra Dee clung on to her girl-midget routine and died the death. Patty Duke, who had been in films at nine, won an Academy Award at sixteen and had her own TV show at seventeen, dumped her wholesome image at the advanced age of twenty-three and tried to relaunch herself as a crazy, mixed-up, sexed-up kid in 1969's *Me Natalie*. It was a rotten flop and heralded Miss Duke's retirement; if there is one thing America doesn't like it's people who step out of their stereotypes.

The hippie way of life received saturation coverage in both the serious and sensationalist media of the late Sixties and early Seventies and made American parents long for the good old days of James Dean and juvenile delinquency, when worst fears centred around underage drinking and staying out past curfew. Now there were *drugs* – thought to be Un-American but suddenly everywhere – for disaffected kids to express their rebellion with, and the problem was suddenly not so much that a teenager would stay out late as the fear that he or she might never come home at all. Running away became an epidemic and grisly stories about the hippie destination, Haight-Ashbury, were passed from suburb to suburb like the latest recipe.

Fathers were too busy eyeing their daughters for signs of drug-addiction to get a crush on them. The nymphet seemed a ridiculously outdated concept – 1968's *Candy* starred Ewa Aulin as a sort of Lolita on LSD and played the sex angle as hallucinogenic high camp.

When hippy was all over as a movement, leaving just the debris and the drifters and the drug problem that would never clear and which is now partially decriminalized because offenders are too numerous to prosecute, a few film people who imagined they were being very bold and stretching out a hand across the generation gulf made little films in which *one* hippie girl (not more, more than one and they might murder you and drink your blood and all the other stories) would drift around explaining her philosophy to the best of her limited ability. Deborah Raffin, Barbara Hershey, Kay Lenz, Sissy Spacek – they were usually hitch-hikers with guitars and ghastly names like Ginger and Breezy and they usually accepted a ride with a tired old businessman who they showed the light by displaying their spiritual innocence and sleeping with. Then they would move on, leaving the old cynic reborn and awed at his good fortune. The cosy message was that it took all kinds of people to make a world and that Mr and Mrs Average should give a ride to the next hippy they passed – they might learn something. These films never made much money for the simple reason that most people thought hippies were smelly scum who deserved to be under the car rather than in it.

Young girls returned to being loved or desired, sexless or sluts. As if it had taken almost twenty years since the rebels with a cause for the cinema to admit that children went through stages of loathing their parents, a new school of thought opened up which expressed the opinion that children were often evil and possessed by the Devil anyway, so it was all right for their parents to loathe them back. The Evil Child motif had been touched on before – in the devastating *The Bad Seed* from the Fifties, starring Patty McCormack and never bettered – but never grasped and flogged with such gusto. The instigator this time around was Linda Blair as the chubby and blasphemous child in *The Exorcist*, a film as successful as it was unpleasant.

For those who did not want to plunge head first into the green bile of Blair, Tatum O'Neal emerged in *Paper Moon* to enormous applause and an Oscar at seven. She served as a refuge for an America sick to its stomach over the atrocities it had committed and its abysmal defeat by Communist Vietnam as she took them for a stroll through the Depression which now seemed like the good old days. And although she played a shrewd little shrew, she was the most comfortably asexual child actress ever to hit the screen. Just what the Sandman ordered in a decade when child pornography became common knowledge.

But the plainness which had endeared O'Neal to her early public has been a hindrance as she has grown up. She has made just six films in a

Brooke Shields: not so much a film star, more a shampoo ad

career that has lasted a decade. Her last major film, *Little Darlings*, concerning two precocious pubescents at summer school, hardly swept the boards and what plaudits there were went to her co-star Kirsty McNicholl – no famous father, no early Oscar, just a solid schooling in TV behind her.

There are just not very many films made these days, and the audience is smaller than it has ever been. The public tend not to follow one star's career regardless any more, and no star can afford to be associated with two unsuccessful films in a row without their reputation and reward suffering.

The career of Brooke Shields is a modern career not because of the under-age sex shock – after the *Pretty Baby* publicity had been harvested and invested Brooke Shields beat a retreat to creaking comedies and slushy puppy love – but because she retreated into respectability not through shame but through sound business sense. Having realized that films today are either too insipid or too exploitative, and often both, to capitalize fully on her epic film star potential, Shields has taken the capitalizing into her own hands and earns vast sums of money endorsing shampoo and designer jeans.

She is an unforgettable face (Mrs Teresa Shields claims that Greta Garbo stopped her as she aired the infant Brooke in Central Park and exclaimed, 'That child is devastating! She will go far!') which is not what the films of today want from girls, for their own perverted reasons. She makes her fortune from the market-place rather than from the movies, acting as more of a model for young girls than a screen-dream for old men – her strong features and stature (she is almost six feet tall) seemed to sabotage her paedophile appeal the moment it first burst into the publicity bubble.

If this were the Thirties, Miss Shields would no doubt be the Number One studio's Number One property, immaculately sold and shielded. As it is, the uproar which followed one of her jeans commercials – 'If my Calvin Kleins could talk, I'd be ruined' – and which led to her latest contribution to the TV campaign against smoking being dropped, nicely reflects her schizoid public image and the tremulous tightrope she must walk between the raunchy and the respectable if she wishes to keep those endorsements multiplying.

Teresa Shields' well-publicized drinking problem (and her daughter's equally well-publicized pleas for her to dry out), the way stand-ins are employed for nude shots, her divorced parents and her Catholic religion, her public disapproval of promiscuity and the naked layout she posed for when she was nine – Brooke Shields bears all the marks of a girl without a studio and a sanctuary. Mother rarely knows best.

A girl without a studio could do worse than Woody Allen's stable. With the exception of Robert Altman, Woody Allen is the only movie brat who enjoys seeing girls on film. He has, God forgive him, launched Meryl Streep and Diane Keaton on an unsuspecting world; he snatched Charlotte Rampling, Chelsea expatriate, from the jaws of celluloid junk concerning killer whales; and he reinvented Mariel Hemingway as a respectable name worth dropping after her debut in Everybuff's most loathed movie (and almost my favourite) *Lipstick*. In *Manhattan* Hemingway played the teenage giantess Tracy, a beacon of noble normality in the midst of a morass of neurosis; in *Personal Best* she played an inverted athlete and last year she played Dorothy Stratten, a murdered *Playboy* model, in *Star 80*. Her young girl status seems to be a hurdle safely jumped and her future seems unlikely to contain much shedding of clothes and screaming, practically compulsory for young actresses these days. Working with Woody Allen seems tantamount to an immunization against unemployment.

There is no modern equivalent of AIP, no series of films turned out to appease a ravenous teenage market any more. Occasional films featuring teenage girls of the Seventies and Eighties have emerged – *Foxes*, starring Jodie Foster, which was enjoyable, and *Times Square*, starring Robin Johnson, which was an embarrassment. There have been considerable career opportunities for young actresses in nostalgia flicks – *I Wanna Hold Your Hand* and *Cooley High* taking the rise out of the Sixties, *American Graffiti* and *Slumber Party '57* celebrating the Fifties – in which girls are the fittings and fixtures of a fixation with the mythical good old days, when girls were chaste and chased and challenges or simple sluts, and sex was a vocation and a victory for a boy, not hard work. The most successful and slick nostalgia flick, *Grease*, featured a sixteen-year-old heroine played by a thirty-year-old woman. But the real-life, public purity of Olivia Newton-John only added to the shock of the new in the last reel, and it is doubtful that a real teenager could have pantomimed her jilted wistfulness and jerry-built wantonness more vividly.

My favourite teenage heroine is *Saturday Night Fever*'s Stephanie, the physically graceful, culturally clumsy arriviste who leads John Travolta by the groin out of his dead-end disco into uptown aspiration. She is special because she cannot love the hero; because she loves the city. She confronts Manhattan like a young pretender prizefighter, she wants to scale the skyline like King Kong. The story is special because the girl serves as an example to the boy, a scenario practically illegal in today's morbidly masculinist movies. Stephanie has a BA in growing pains and looks like the Statue of Liberty's smarter younger sister to the baffled boy. It is special, almost a modern big-screen phenomenon, in that the hero recognizes his potential by deserting the gang in favour of one girl rather than escaping the female agent of social control to find true love and liberation with men on motorcycles or crime sprees or search-and-destroy massacres in South-East Asia. Hepburn and Tracy doing the Hustle! – moral superiority and massive success, alive and dancing on the peeling silver screen.

But not for long. Those who indulge in conspiracy theories could manufacture a real lulu around the fact that Karen Lynn Gorney, the creator of the singular Stephanie, has never been seen on the big screen since. Her grandfather wrote the Depression classic 'Brother, Can You Spare A Dime?' and this may yet become her theme. Miss Gorney is probably unemployed because prospective employers identify her with Stephanie – too spirited to be easily led, to be easily chased and terrorized and killed. Too alive to die easily.

For most young actresses these days make a living from dying, at least nine times like a cat. Cutting up once took place in the cutting room; now it is man's favourite onscreen sport. From goddess to garbage – from vamp to...

Chapter Ten
VICTIM

How do they kill you? Let me count the ways — oh, I give up! *Why* do they kill you? Pick your own alibi. Fake blood is cheap; it's quicker than writing sharp dialogue (and besides, they don't have the wit); they're sick and they reckon in tried and true All-American style that they may as well sell their sickness on the open market; it's What The Public Wants (despite the fact that audiences are declining as rapidly as ever).

Why has carnage colonized the big screen? Perhaps people hide in pretend horror in times when real horror is rife, a childish and wishful response, the pretend horror being popular because you can walk away knowing that the victims screamed all the way to the bank. Perhaps the audience would like to commit violence upon their friends and neighbours but do not want to go to jail. Perhaps the white world's guilt has at last caught up with it and all it wants to do is wallow in dreams of death until it blows itself up — the big suicide.

Screen violence is respectable now in a way that screen sex will never be. Violence, in the death-wish society, is somehow *clean*, despite the fact that blood and guts make much more of a mess on the carpet than the pale by-products of sex. You must join private clubs or go to grubby ghettos to see certain aspects of celluloid sex; there are no private violence film-clubs, because violence in its most gratuitous forms can find a place on the big screen.

Sex is 'cleansed' by violence in the mind of the middle-aged movie brat, it seems, and the sex which stands the best chance of getting into a film these days is rape, which can be justified by censors and other sick ruling minds as less harmful to public morals than straightforward and consenting lust — because rape shows sex as an undesirable experience for a woman, and therefore is not conducive to the corruption and arousal of a nation's future wives and mothers. As for the effect that violent sex as the celluloid norm might have on male audiences – well, as the Bible and boastful folk-lore has it, men are in such a constant state of animal rampancy (which may come as a surprise to the wealthy purveyors of sex aids and the harassed agony aunts endlessly consoling sex-starved wives) that such displays of aggression make little difference.

War films, westerns – in the past men have watched these, bloodless folk-tales and lies that served their purpose for those too dim to read history. But now these films are few and far between and the cinema chronicles and perpetuates the undeclared post-War war, the war on the ultimate underclass, the servant's servant, the slave's slave – women. Post-War Western man feels somewhat drained and debilitated by his monument-ally soft life, and knows he is in no shape to take on the Enemy or the Indians if they come rolling into West Berlin or riding round the mountain. Yet in his slack state he feels the need more than ever to establish his divine right of domination over some strata; what better target than the enemy within, acting up something awful, demanding dangerous privileges like a decent wage. As girls become more combative on the street, they are increasingly shown as victims on the screen.

The sound of screaming has always shrieked through cinemas to some extent, but until now it was not the inevitable end of any bright young thing with a wiggle in her walk and a giggle in her talk. In the early Thirties Tod Browning filmed *Dracula*. The film's fatalistic acceptance of the super-natural hit a nerve in one of the waves of humdrum hysteria that ripple incessantly around Fortress America, and its massive success caused a mad rummage through Poe's, Stevenson's and Shelley's black-edged back pages. One daring cinema proprietor double-featured Transylvania's treasure and Frankenstein's monster, laying on a doctor, nurses and an ambulance to add to the suspense and anticipation.

These stories are set in Eastern Europe and so had a ready-made audi-ence in early twentieth-century America, people eager to hide in the old half-remembered, half-mocked horror of Vlad the Impaler rather than look at the new horror of Hitler.

Britain has never been half as civilized as it liked to think – witch-burning, pig-sticking, cock-fighting, the hunting of anything beautiful – and by Elizabethan times there was a taste for theatrical gore. Dis-embowelling was a popular spectacle: a sheep's stomach would be sewn up and put inside an actor's clothes so that when he was 'stabbed' on stage the audience would get an eyeful of entrails. Now Britain, chaperoned by Hammer Films, took to Dracula. Why – because he appeared a gentleman? Maybe Transylvania was a far-flung Imperial outpost and the Count was out there keeping an eye-tooth on things...Anyhow, Hammer hatched dozens of Dracula flicks throughout the Fifties, Sixties and Seventies. My personal favourite was *Dracula AD 1972* which followed the fangs and fortunes of a distant relation, one Johnny Alucard (Get it? A backward glance will do...) and the wilful gang of King's Road coffee bar kids he ensnares, including such great second-wind Swinging London faces as Marsha 'Hair' Hunt and Caroline 'Navy Rum' Munro. Like AIP on the beach, they were slick and successful and sure of their market at a time when cinemas were a cinch for rebirth as bingo parlours.

Unlike the Beach Party films, Hammer Horrors ran the gamut from the garbage to the almost great – some of them were every bit as good as Roger Corman's grandiose American efforts. You could not be sure who would get bitten and who would survive. They were just predictable enough – you could be sure of a big no-expense-or-red-paint-spared, stake-through-the-heart smorgasbord at the end and you could be sure that a lot of attractive girls would bare their throats to the man in the cloak before the lights went up.

In the early Hammer Horrors the bitten would be ladies – usually played by Maxine Audley or Hazel Court – who never knew what nibbled them and could somehow be retrieved from phantom to fiancée in the last reel, but as the Sixties swung on, a platoon of pleasant peasant girls were brought in to show more chest and lust – eternal starlets like Veronica Carlson and the late Imogen Hassall. Like the Beach Parties, you could build a career in Hammer Horrors; like the Beach Parties, they were often the only work available to down-at-heel film stars. Joan Collins, after the Hollywood build-up and break-up of her prime, screamed her way through tales from the crypt too numerous to mention until her little sister's books bailed her out.

Although the Hammer Horrors showed less flesh than a bikini, they were more sexual; the throat is a neglected thing of beauty and the act of baring it to famished fangs was a provocative and predatory gesture that stayed on the safe side of the censor's scissors where a spoken invitation could be cut. No one ever went to a Hammer Horror to see men biting girls because there was simply nothing to see: the Count and the cloak and the camera knew that less was more and conspired to those elegant ends. The one carve-up you could count on was the stake-out at the end – the Count out for the count.

These were poor people's fairy-tales, very innocent – victims were incidental window-dressing. But while the poor people were watching Hammer Horrors the critics had developed a collective crush on Alfred Hitchcock, to whom the victim was the pivot of a film, as essential as a clapperboard. He was the first British film director to make an art out of exploiting his own sickness for profit and applause and it was he who spiritually spawned the current crop of Americans to whom women are things to be hurt, hunted and hacked to death. Hell hath no fury like a physically repellent reject with a director's chair.

When people speak of the Hitchcock heroine they are describing Grace Kelly: blonde, blank, something in the bank, running rings round some regular Joe and acting like royalty a long time before she actually was. Kelly – as used in three films – and Eva Marie Saint (how Hitchcock must have loved that name – class and chastity!) were these. They may have been humbled a little and taught to walk at heel by Cary Grant, but they would never be torn by birds or blades because starch ran in their veins and they were unimpeachably *ladies* and ultimately indestructible, as their class appears to the working-class Tory (a tribe of which Hitch was a fully paid-up member – a sort of psychopathic, arty Alf Garnett). The early English heroines, girls like Madeleine Carroll and Ann Todd, were treated with even more reserve; the attitude was chummy and chivalrous. Ingrid Bergman was given the pride of place in a pigeonhole all her own – a fat man's Garbo, all suffering and sacrifice and stolid Swedish somnambulism. When drunk, Hitchcock would boast to impressionable journalists that Bergman had been 'in love with me for thirty years. Mad for me all her life' – which seems impossible, to say the least.

Hitchcock's wrath is reserved for the girls in the films that mark the turning of the Fifties into the Sixties – Tippi Hedren, Janet Leigh and Kim Novak, who are not teased but terrorized. These Bad Blondes are given some ridiculously token character flaw – stealing, sassiness, selfishness – so that Hitchcock's retribution can be righteous. The retribution *always* takes the form of physical assault; Hitchcock seems ill-at-ease in a century that does not exercise the stocks and the ducking-stool.

Sometimes his slimy internal sickness seeps out too far and shocks even the sloppy censor: the murder of Marion in *Psycho* was originally composed of *fourteen* stabbings and was cut to four.

In the Bad Blonde films, a beautiful brunette always stands by – Suzanne Pleshette, Diane Baker – so that the Bad Blonde can be killed without the hero having to go home alone. In the Classy Blonde films *she* is the only female focus, a sign of reassurance to the audience that nothing of lasting damage will happen to her. But Hitchcock himself became addicted to the routine bloodletting of his Sixties' films and never returned to the elegant fencing of his Fifties' jigsaws. Maybe he thought he was moving with the times, that the audience was no longer worthy of energetic plots – preferring the massacre to the maze every time. He no longer crafted vehicles fit for his female ideal, who ceased to exist as Hitchcock decided that the market-place was now no place to take a lady. His female ideal's physiognomy was for hire in the Sixties, too, in the shape of Candice Bergen, who made Grace Kelly look like an Irish navvy – but Hitchcock never approached her. The faceless corpses of *Frenzy* were the dog-ends of his desire, and all he thought he deserved.

Golden girl, Gothic boy: Tate and Polanski

Alfred Hitchcock was a waddling testimony to the guilt-gouged religion of Rome; Pope Innocent as playground bully. He delighted in dishing out dirt – making money from marketing murder, calling actors 'cattle' (his stupid appearances, which he claimed the public loved, were his brand, no doubt), cutting Kim Novak's legs from *Vertigo* on the grounds that they were thick – but was incapable of taking it.

Tippi Hedren, *Marnie* and Melanie in *The Birds*, was Hitchcock's last big project. He planned to make a star of her, as he had in his dreams of Bergman and Kelly. One day Miss Hedren teased her slovenly Svengali about something that stuck out a mile – his gut. He never featured her in a film again and her career was left barely breathing.

People tend to behave badly in foreign countries, be they football fans or film moguls with a fantasy. Hitchcock, an English Catholic, treated American glacier girls very badly when he got the upper hand; you could hardly expect a Polish Jew to treat them like priceless porcelain.

Roman Polanski was very well-behaved in post-War Poland, as citizens of Communist countries are apt to be. He had been hidden by teenage Communist partisans as a child, and with them he had linked up with the Russian Army poised to take Cracow. He had accepted the consumer durables the Russians rewarded him with – his proudest possession was a bicycle – and he had let the State put him through film school. He finally went to the West because the draft was coming up and because Communism did not allow 'artistic freedom' – freedom meaning buckets of blood, that well-known human right. Ah, artistic licence, what crimes are committed in your name! Polanski settled in Paris and moved on to America only when the question of French military service arose.

Malice in Wonderland. He married the most gorgeous slab of Americana at hand – Sharon Tate, starlet, Army brat, ex-Miss Tiny Tot of Dallas, late of Washington and Texas – more American than napalm! He made his films with artistic freedom; like Hitchcock, he liked to place genteel blondes – Catherine Deneuve, Mia Farrow, Faye Dunaway, Francesca Annis – dazed and defenceless on urban battlefields. Like de Sade, he liked to tell tales in which the only women who avoided victimization were women who drew the first blood. The most shocking moment of *Rosemary's Baby* is when Farrow drops the knife and in doing so is doomed to rear the Devil. The women who save their skins lose their minds anyway and wander red-handed around elegant abattoirs, bloody and beautiful, zombie trophies.

Occasionally, as though to reassure himself and the world that he's just jolly old John Doe beneath the tortured mask, Polanski tried to make a 'comedy'. The bubonic plague raised more laughs than a Polanski comedy; *Dance Of The Vampires* starred Sharon Tate and *Que?* starred Sydne Rome – Polanski's only Jewish sex interest – being cute and confused. Both were spectacular failures, rubbing in the sad fact that what people wanted from

Polanski was blood — hold the flesh.

Polanski has lived more from the profits of public interest in his private life — the escape from the ghetto, the flight from Communism, the slaughter of his wife, the running from America to escape the juvenile sex scandal — than from the fruits of his films. He is a mildly talented blood-hound, but without the crates of ketchup he is as clueless as an actor without a script. Slashed arteries for art's sake!

Polanski's baby died with Sharon Tate — but he would eventually, with Hitchcock, beget many heirs. No one is quicker to jump on the art band-wagon when it aims to push back the taboo frontier than the sickos and the exploiters; they fraternize and miscegenate and before long it is hard to tell who's who. Art caught exploitation and exploitation caught art.

The main legacy that Hitchcock and Polanski passed on, like concerned parents, was DON'T TALK TO STRANGERS. It was *people* who were the monsters now, people who looked like you and bore no identifying mark such as a black cloak or a bolt through the neck. The innocent folk-tales of the Thirties were laughable stuff compared to a five-minute news bulletin; in the debris of the Longest Party, in the first years of the Seventies, people looked around and felt scared. Crime took over from sex as the Western worry; everyone was doing it but you!

1971 saw *A Clockwork Orange* and *Straw Dogs*, both supposedly made to show the undesirability of violence, but of course no one believed *that* old

Straw Dogs: Susan George suffers in silence

chestnut apart from Messrs Kubrick and Peckinpah's moms. Susan George, pop-eyed starlet acting as the pouting target in *Straw Dogs*, was the first girl to build a career of sorts out of being a punch-bag. In the years 1970-71 she shrieked her way through *Die Screaming, Marianne, Fright* and *Sudden Terror* (the subtlety of the titles is what tickles me). Hayley Mills also possessed the requisite wide eyes and bruisable baby face and so was a cinch for such screamers as *Twisted Nerve, Endless Night* and *Deadly Strangers*. In *Play Misty For Me* a girl maniac tracks a *man* – but don't worry, his loyal love interest is around to take the actual physical abuse in the last reel.

In retrospect, the battered blondes of the early Seventies were really rather well treated. 'Retrospect' means having turned tired eyes away from the cruelty-without-beauty boom that has lasted from the late Seventies until now. These films do not just depend on having a girl used as berserk-bait; they depend on having a *series* of girls, no more distinguishable from each other than skittles. Susan George and Hayley Mills played victims with names, traits, personas (in *Endless Night* Hayley Mills is the sixth richest woman in the world!) who get away by the skin of their capped teeth to hide their eyes in the hero's shoulder while the predator plunges to his death.

The teenagers of *The Texas Chainsaw Massacre, Prom Night, The Fog, Terror Train, Friday The 13th* and *Halloweens 1* and *2* are totally interchangeable – giggly, vacuous, boy-crazy – and they must be punished for growing into the very thing they have been raised as, All-American girls. They are invariably unmarried, which shows a great respect for the property laws – in *He Knows You're Alone* the high-principled killer gets in there just in time and kills girls the night before they marry. Even the famished fish of *Jaws* wasn't all bad; if you run around in a bikini you're fit for nothing but being a shark snack, but the dutiful beautiful police chief's wife is the girl who gets away.

The actresses who appear in these films are dually disposable – on screen and in memory. Only a couple of names stick in the mind: Nancy Allen, who is married to gore-galore director Brian De Palma (they're sort of an ugly and untalented Tate and Polanski), and Jamie Lee Curtis who occasionally survives the line-up-to-be-strangled screamers. Her appeal is twofold; she is skinny, serious and not of the hated cheerleader breed – and she is the daughter of Tony Curtis and – gulp – JANET LEIGH! Hellish heaven – to direct JANET LEIGH's daughter and pretend you're the *Master* choreographing the shower-stall stabbing!

Hitchcock's bad influence on these ringmasters can also be seen in De Palma's *Dressed To Kill* – the transvestite as terrorist, the Thing that chases every little Catholic boy through his nightmares!

Why are these screaming teen films so popular? Well, the audience – the majority are between seventeen and twenty-five – have not mortgaged away their box-office money yet and like to see films about their own kind. Physically repellent directors like to make films about girls being literally crushed to pay back for all the times when *they* were metaphorically crushed by girls as acned adolescents. They can be made on the cheap by hiring bad actors desperate for jobs. They make what is considered to be a crock of gold in these dog days – *Friday The 13th* grossed twenty million dollars in a month. Maybe the sickness of the father is visited on the son.

Even in the market-place of the arty, the sophisticated and the redneck, the victim boom bloomed. *Tattoo* found Maud Adams as a promiscuous model kidnapped and tattooed from head to toe by a lunatic who, the film all but announced as a finale, *had taught the shallow slut a thing or two about real devotion by the time the toxics got her. Looking For Mr Goodbar* pretended to pray for the prey of the singles bars, but the sign language said *this is what you get if you don't sit at home sewing HOME SWEET HOME samplers.*

And the victim-as-catalyst stopped Michael Winner from having to re-name himself Michael Loser after a decade of dunces when he started making the *Death Wish* films; Charles Bronson, liberal, finds his wife/mother/daughter/sister/pet female parakeet raped and murdered and goes on a one-man springclean with a sub-automatic machine gun. The savages are, inevitably, black – imagine *Birth Of A Nation* with Bronx accents. These films are spectacularly successful; the audience stands up and cheers when Bronson, driven berserk beyond belief, blows another sewer-rat away. Though I know they are cheering the killing of a black rather than the killing of a killer.

When in 1980 Al Pacino played a policeman who goes deep into the sub-terranean show-and-sell lifestyle of the leather homosexual in order to investigate a series of invert murders, homosexuals picketed cinemas showing *Cruising* and the film was a flop – even more indicative of distress, it did not spawn a sequel, almost compulsory for any new twist on violence.

Women, despite their massive numbers, do not picket the latest chase-and-kill films in great numbers. A few took a pot-shot at *Dressed To Kill*, but not enough to make people turn away. Women's stupid acceptance of themselves as naturals for the victim revival reflects the two-kinds-of-woman myth they have been sold by men; oh, they're talking about a *different* kind of woman, they're raping a *different* kind of woman – not *me.* Homosexuals, for all their faults, tend not to divide themselves into good or bad, some worthy of killing and others worthy of respect – therefore they have clout.

Will violence ever stop being the biggest box-office draw, or is it the terminus of Western taste? Well, it has a lot on its side; liberals and the media incline towards the slick lie that cinematic violence is a mirror, not a starting-block, to society.

Yet it is invariably *young women* — girls in their late teens and early twenties — who are raped and culled. In the real world, the rape and slaughter of very young girl children and very old women has increased horrifically as young women toughen up; if the cinema really *was* a mirror, these atrocities would appear in big-screen plots. Yet the director and the consumer *do not want* this inconvenient fact, it would be *sick*. Thus is the butchering of young women declared healthy and sellable and sexy. The mirror cracks.

Another boost to the market value of mayhem is the stupidity of actors. By their very nature — wanting to spend a lifetime speaking other people's words rather than their own? Describe *that* to a Martian and see his disbelief — actors are ciphers, and in studio days heroic personas were fed into their empty souls. Post-studio, après-Actor's Studio, the stupid actor wants to *streeetch* himself; being a nice guy, he wants to play a bad guy. He attempts to flout Hannah Arendt's fact, 'the banality of evil', by proving the *carnality* of evil.

As Uncle Andy said, 'Bonnie and Clyde didn't look like Faye and Warren' — neither did the Boston Strangler look like Tony Curtis, Caryl Chessman look like Alan Alda nor Gary Gilmore look like Tommy Lee Jones, yet these are the faces that the paying public will come to stick on the actual scum.

Suicides are infinitely more varied and interesting people, but glamorous actors do not rush to play them, despite their desire to be stretched. Suicide lacks a certain aggression, *action* — violence has become a sex substitute once more and suicide would look too much like masturbation — *you can't find anyone to do it to*. The modern marketing of murder is a boy's own, man's game — imagine an attractive young actress announcing that she was interested in playing, say, Myra Hindley...she would probably be committed to an asylum on the spot. Does it matter that violence-voyeurism is the vice that dare speak its name? Well, I think so. Films of extreme cruelty are most popular in West Germany and Japan — cultures I would not trust to be in the healthiest states of mind, *minds that want revenge*. Is it wrong that the cinema, which once worked to enlighten, now works to *wallow*? Just what is the point of showing even more slime to a sick society?

The point, the anti-censorship monolith will bleat here, is *freedom*. Ah, yes, precious Western freedom; the freedom that people died to preserve, were tortured for rather than tell things that might imperil freedom, walked into certain death in the name of. The freedom the West waves in the face of Communism as its only advantage; the freedom to speak, assemble, believe and all that jazz. And let us not forget the sacred modern freedom, the freedom given to us lucky people by the great god Video — the freedom to watch *The Evil Dead* in the privacy of one's own free home without the fear of infringement...

Chapter Eleven
THREE GIRLS

By now millions of girls have run to Hollywood; thousands have been groomed by studios; hundreds have starred in films. Only three have become legendary to the point where their surnames are more like trademarks than real names: Garbo, Monroe, Bardot.

It is not just because they were beautiful – Rita Hayworth at her peak leaves them all standing. They *touched nerves*, and tapped them for desire, which is why their names will never be abandoned as bywords of a particular need. They all have alliterative initials, but so did Diana Dors and Kay Kendall. They shared blonde beauty, but that is practically par for the film-star course. Their blonde beauty was their disguise and beneath it, like a file in a cake, they carried their real merchandise: Garbo the holy whore, Monroe the baby girl, and Bardot the Casanova man.

When the capitalist West is wretched and ragged and deep in the clutches of yet another depression, it comforts itself that at least it is not socialistic like Sweden *where everybody commits suicide because things are so soft*. The West conveniently ignores the fact that *its* suicide rate goes up rapidly every time capitalism has a dizzy spell and starts an epidemic of unemployment, whereas Sweden's is stable; it also pretends it doesn't know that those bastions of free enterprise, Switzerland, Austria and Japan, have suicide rates which make Sweden look like a picture of health.

In the sixteenth century, Sweden dominated Finland and Germany, but by the eighteenth century its imperial illness was over and it kept itself to itself. It has not had a war since 1814. It possesses marvellous natural resources and the high standard of living goes hand in hand with the high level of socialization (even the alcohol industry is State-owned) far too easily to let fellow Westerners sleep easily and dream of the downfall of socialism at night. The only thing that the West can comfort itself with is

Garbo: gloomy ambassador of suicidal Sweden

the myth that Sweden is *boring* – hence the tired old suicide line; though why the rate of exodus from Sweden is so low if it is so slow, no one knows – and even if it never produces any human debris and State-hating terrorists like, say, West Germany does, on the other hand it does not produce any world-beaters.

I am at a loss to think of any post-War idols that West Germany, following this freedom-to-fall-or-rise argument, has given the planet. Sweden, though, has the habit of exploding maverick novas, from Jenny Lind through Bjorn Borg to Abba, spectacularly and singularly successful in their chosen field.

And Garbo, gloomy ambassador of suicide, holder of the *Litteris et Artibus* for services to Sweden. A film star who went against every code of behaviour the film star commits herself to when she reveals her ambition (her lack of temperament, her four almost-marriages rather than the usual four divorces, her loathing of publicity), Garbo has made every film star since look something of a sap. Her humourlessness has endeared her to every intellectual of the post-War world, where it can be seen as something prophetic and terrible. Something in her face rings a bell with everyone under the shadow of the Bomb, from the American students who reject rock concerts in favour of Garbo revivals to the Italian public of 1962 whose cinema audiences decreased by over *seventy-five per cent* when a clutch of her films were shown on TV.

From the start of her career – 'I want to be let alone' – to the end – 'I have been dead for years' – there has been something unconstitutional about Garbo. In her face one sees the cynicism she must have felt when she learned that the pursuit of happiness was a written rule of American life. Physically she was some ultimate in evolution, as finely-drawn and un-animal as it seems possible to be; in the same way she was the bringer of *angst*, mass melancholy, in a way that the human race does not seem able to move on from.

Thus was the bringer of bad news killed over and over again on the screen – the foreigner fatale with the altar eyes and temple hair. Beautiful, clever, cultured, calm *and* sexually available – the combination that America could never crack or control or ever admit the existence of again.

On screen, Garbo died time and time again, to reassure America that the foreign power was mortal, and she lives on today; on screen, Monroe must never be allowed to die, to prove that America and little girls last for ever, and today she is dead.

A cannibal's cordon bleu – it is a shame that the most lovable film star ever should attract men for all the wrong reasons; men who love a victim, men who like stupid women, men who love little girls. Paedophilia had a field day in Marilyn, with her oop-poop-a-doop and her da-da-daddies. The really young girls, Tuesday Weld and Sue Lyon, looked *wise* – they played bitches, basically, who'd ruin you in the end, just like a woman. Marilyn was all for your pleasure – she made little men feel big.

Saint Marilyn! – she was too *done to* to bear responsibility for all the sex slurs that came out after she had gone to sleep the sleep of the innocent – abortionists' beds, casting couches. She suffered! She was punished! She can go to heaven! It is the victim in her that appeals to drag queens and male intellectuals – one and the same, aren't they? Norman Mailer is the archetype, with his dreams of wet sex but even wetter (and so sexier) death – Marilyn as crucifixée on locker room wall, Marilyn as Los Angeles County Coroner's Case No. 81128 – but no time or love for the woman who was the nucleus of the creature. Mailer, incidentally, gave his old adversary the US quite a PR job when he claimed that Marilyn typifies America to the foreigner: Mansfield does it much better – something ugly which thinks it is beautiful, something which thinks it is on top even as it crumbles to dust.

A face made of milk and honey from a land made of muck and money: MM

Capitalism loves a Cinderella story, the one in a million who proves that America is, if not a land of opportunity, then at least a land of opportunism. From madness and illegitimacy and poverty, through an orphanage where Cinderella was paid five cents a month for scrubbing lavatories, through cutting room floors and nude calendars and cheesecake, to stardom to — well, loneliness and madness and suicide. The unwritten end of the Cinderella story.

If Marilyn had been allowed to act herself on screen, as women did when American men weren't afraid of their own shadow and their own Mom and the Russians, if she had been allowed to embroider on her own personality as film stars did from Crawford to Gardner, she might have been happy. It would have worked, too. She was something much more sympathetic than a social-climber or a gypsy, she was a girl who lived for that final love and used mass love as a last resort.

She played stupid girls who thought they were smart but she was a smart girl who thought she was stupid. She played gold-diggers while giving blank cheques to the Actor's Studio. She played girls to whom everything came easily, but she had things hard, even when her beauty was evident. She played creatures brimming over with juicy hormones — wet eyes, licked lips, skin like milk-filled silk — but her life seemed to be one constant miscarriage.

In death Marilyn has become strangely sexless — she is a MARILYN, a species apart. In life she was a man's woman because men wanted her; now she is a man's woman because a lot of men want to be her. For lots of girls she is a way of making a living. Marilyn Monroe is impersonated by Marilyn Marshall in nightclubs, Debbie Arnold on television, Linda Kerridge in commercials, Misty Rowe, Catherine Hicks, Tracey Gold and Theresa Russell on film — Sheree North, the very blonde brought in by Fox to scare Marilyn back into line in the last stages of her career, has given a good performance as Gladys Baker, Norma Jean's mother. Even an original like the crooner Deborah Harry could be found claiming that Marilyn was her real mother circa 1978 — such a boast was guaranteed to grab a headline or two.

The Monroe industry in recent years has mutated into the Monroe crusade — an attempt by a crack élite of worshippers to help the memory transform the sad and sorry self-death in the cheap hacienda, a death with dirty toenails on grubby sheets, an orphanage death, into an *assassination*, a noble death in the Sixties Stateside style by the forces of All-American evil, the CIA — to help Marilyn up from between Carole Landis and Jean Seberg into the rarified air of Kings and Kennedys. Even twenty years after her death, kind men are *trying to help her* — and the vulnerability that provokes this response in kind men provokes a kinkier response in unkind men, and so really is not a clever thing to cultivate.

153

BB: which beast belongs behind bars?

Monroe's successor and spiritual antithesis is Brigitte Bardot — the sex kitten who became the cat that walked alone. Although a definitive blonde, Bardot is an emotional (not to mention a natural) brunette — free-wheeling, amoral, swashbuckling, like Liz or Ava or Gina. Garbo's blonde-ness is pulled back in a barette and sleeked down so as not to spoil the purity of her perfect Olympian silhouette; Monroe's blondeness is ash and impeccable, a cross between a gun moll and a baby girl, neither straight nor curly but softly waved, soft like her body and her soul. Bardot's hair is dyed for Vadim's sake and then just left to hang, in a way that a beautiful girl's hair has never been allowed to hang before on the big screen. Bardot has obviously just walked out of the cabana, not the coiffeur's.

Ambition is very American — and very un-French. The French are very smug, which may come of their having had an empire *and* a revolution; like measles, people believe these things only happen once. It is fitting that *bourgeois* is a French word, because a lot of French people fit the description.

French film actresses, like British ones, tend to come from bourgeois homes, and so, like British girls, they rarely have the drive that leads to international success. They prefer to *live* rather than act and pour all their energy into their private lives. Catherine Deneuve, Françoise Dorleac, Jeanne Moreau, Simone Simon, Juliette Greco, Mylene Demongeot, Michele Morgan, Danielle Darrieux, Martine Carol — all very beautiful and all very insular, believing that the world begins and ends with La France. Even Simone Signoret, accepted by the international film world to the point of three Oscars, has never accepted the international film world.

But the word 'Bardot' is Esperanto and although she is the most insular — almost xenophobic — of the lot, she is also a legend. And unlike Garbo and Monroe, she has attained this status with no sacrifice of her private and physical lives.

Her attachment to one place — the sun and sand and sea of Saint Tropez — and her impatience anywhere else shows strong roots of the kind most film stars would give their false nails for. She has always enjoyed men too much to fall prey to the starlet's disease — being an old man's darling and precious little else — and has been loving and leaving boys since her early twenties (she is older now, but the boys are still the same age). She has always had a phrase which she applies to all but the very youngest of men — it would translate as 'ready for chrysanthemums'.

On screen she stars confidently with other, often younger, women — Jane Birkin, Jeanne Moreau, Claudia Cardinale — and when she stars with men her *leaving* is in sharp contrast to Monroe's searching and Garbo's fatalism. And what other sex symbol, dependent on the goodwill of men for her popularity, would dare speak the line, 'Men are passé — useless!'

Her healthiness is perhaps most in evidence considering her glorious anti-Americanism. Her rejection of Hollywood's promises came to a head with *Dear Brigitte*, a film about an eight-year-old American genius (surely a contradiction in terms?) whose world revolves around his idol. Bardot was offered ten thousand pounds — a lot in 1965 — for five minutes' work. She would not leave France. Eventually the complete cast and crew, including James Stewart, were forced to pack up and go to France for their costly five minutes of film. Bardot had made the mountain move to the Mademoiselle. (A little later Bardot was angry to find that her *Viva Maria!* contract included a clause promising that she would visit the US for publicity purposes. She went, but the spirit was unwilling; 'Who is Hedda Hopper?' she asked innocently in her hotel room while Hopper furiously got drunk and waited down in the bar.)

Do these three girls – servants and symbols of special needs – share anything but pulchritude and peroxide? Well, none of them retired at their peak,
although we charitably remember them as doing so. Garbo's films made a
profit only in Europe; Monroe had just had a terrible turkey in the shape of
The Misfits and Bardot's fee had slipped to fifteenth highest in the French
cinema (Alain Delon, the first, earned five times more), but they did at least
leave looking good, each in her own way. They did not subject us to their
once-beautiful faces hoisted so high on their heads by the surgeon's skill
that a smile is an impossibility akin to flying in the sky. They did not descend
to TV or hardcore or scream-bore, dragging the love of fans with them
until the fan is forced to laugh and lie, 'I never really loved her.'

It is also interesting that none of them have had visible children: Monroe
and Garbo in reality, Bardot in effect. But Bardot did have a baby with her
second husband, the young, beautiful and neurotic actor Jacques Charrier,
three years her junior. But from the day he left hospital, Nicolas Bardot had
his own apartment next door to his mother's home – the youngest citizen
of France to be head of a household. When Bardot and her husband divorced, Charrier was voluntarily given custody by Bardot. Despite this, Bardot
had the most technically beautiful body; Garbo was inclined to be flat of
foot and chest while Monroe walked the narrow line between bountiful
and bulging. Only Bardot appeared naked on the screen; only Bardot
appears prone in the mind's eye. She was created to lie on a bed or a beach
– Bardot on her feet is as foreign as the Eiffel Tower on its side.

Despite the universal worship of the Madonna myth, the world has seen
a few mothers since then, and is somewhat cynical about them – bad
mothers, bored mothers, battering mothers. Subconsciously, Western
societies feel that procreating is the easy option for women who cannot
create something tangible, something fit to compete in the masculine
market-place. Society can blather on all it likes about the sanctity of
motherhood, but the girls on film it has always worshipped – not just this
trinity but all the fictions – are ritually removed from humdrum women by
their sexy sterility. Even the ultimate 'family' film, *The Sound Of Music*, (*The
Sound Of Money*, the sharks sneered enviously when it gatecrashed Swinging 1965 and walked out with 135 million dollars), boasts a heroine who
acts as a mother to the swoony Captain's seven children, but is not – better
still, she is a nun!

From the poorest common denominator to the most pretentious, there is
just *something there*, some organism living in the triangle of eyes and
mouth that traps the intellectual every time. Do you think that de Beauvoir
would have eulogized, say, Deneuve, Mailer Mansfield or Kenneth Tynan
Britt Ekland if there weren't? More to the point, would *I*?

Chapter Twelve
HURRICANE LIZ

'I always swore I wouldn't end up like Judy' — Elizabeth Taylor

Actors are not easy people to like — female actors less so, but all the same. It is not so much that they give themselves airs as give themselves neuroses. Because they are glorified, all but the brightest feel guilt, and even the happy, laughing ones — take Natalie Wood — turn out to have, if not a skeleton in the closet, then a complete spectrum of mood-altering drugs in the bathroom cabinet. Until now I have given no actress star-billing because the usual catalogues of neglect and regret I would be forced to refer to would bore me and you. Elizabeth Taylor, however, is compulsive and something completely different.

Elizabeth Taylor is a cavewoman. She has never been to a psychiatrist. She is known beyond the English-speaking world along with Muhammad Ali, Winston Churchill and Coca Cola. Unlike other stars of her calibre, she has never possessed that certain frigidity and fright of life that fame feeds on. She has had it all — children, grandchildren, Oscars, diamonds, the most expensive film ever made, animals and husbands — and she has been it all — a star, an actress, a wife, a mother, a grandmother, a beauty, a Jew, the highest paid entertainer in the world, the first star to receive a million dollars for one film, a philanthropist and public enemy. She has acted as a modern Hogarth fable, an illustration of how to commit the Seven Deadly Sins in style and she is GREAT. She is Mother Courage, unforgivable or unforgettable depending on your love of life; like Napoleon, her history is irresistible — 'How did she *get* like that?'

Elizabeth Taylor was born in Golders Green in 1932. Her mother was fair, of German extraction; her father was dark, of Scottish and English origin; they were both Kansans. Yet they crossed the world to create a child in

ET: Girl From Planet X

Golders Green, the Jewish heartland of England. It was not quite a stable, but it would do for the woman who would become the most famous Jewess in the world.

She was taken back to America to hide from the War and when she was ten she showed up at MGM to audition for the first *Lassie* film. On hearing her voice, Louis B. Mayer decreed that the other children be sent home.

Mayer worshipped Britain, primarily for their stand against Nazi Germany, which he kindly mistook for protectiveness towards the Jews. To him, Britain was beautiful *and* box-office – his ideal of sex-appeal was showy but starchy Greer Garson, who as Mrs Miniver won eight Academy Awards for Mayer's studio as well as stirring Roosevelt to war second only to Pearl Harbour. Elizabeth Taylor immediately struck him as a world-beater with her facial beauty and phonetic Britishness. As late as 1948, when Taylor had moved prematurely to romantic leads as beautiful and rich American girls due to the enormous bosom she had grown at fifteen, the publicity hand-out bragged, 'Elizabeth Taylor is as British as they come.'

The rules were always changed by Elizabeth Taylor, right back in MGM's Little Red Schoolhouse. Her breasts were not bound down, as was the custom with lucrative child stars, but put straight into the best uplift money could buy. She was an established star before the menarche; not for her the hopeful starlet touting of wares that sows the seeds of self-hatred. And at sixteen she looked like a king-maker: see Philippe Halsman's vision in the gold dress – probably, no, DEFINITELY, the last word on beauty. Taylor looks at the camera like a bullfighter without a weapon, her beauty both red rag and shining armour. Being a sixteen-year-old sex goddess no doubt had its contradictions, but Taylor preferred to air them sarcastically rather than let them fester – 'How,' she asked a friend, 'am I supposed to concentrate on my education when Robert Taylor keeps sticking his tongue down my throat?'

The more the studio harped on her classiness, the more Taylor dressed like a floosie. She loved low necklines and heavy make-up, bubble gum and cigarettes. When a camera came near her she arched her back and put her best breast forward. In the late Forties there was a fashion for very tight belts dividing full swirly skirts and tight sweaters: even resident nice girls like Jane Powell followed it. But there are some women who are constructed so that even an innocent inhalation looks like an attempt to solicit. Elizabeth Taylor was one of them. When she walked into the MGM canteen in a tight belt, a massive and involuntary gasp echoed through the huge room.

What did she look like by now? The foreigner remodelled; a creature from a planet where the races are one. Classic features, lustrous Jewish hair and that satin Latin skin. And those eyes, those twin badges of Otherness!

And that name, the kind of schoolmarmy name that Hitchcock would have gone into a sweat upon hearing while running a mile from the dark flesh-pot it belonged to — ELIZABETH TAYLOR! — so far from the languid Ritas and Lanas and Avas. And that body, a natural wonder like a mountain range; not something smelling suspiciously of silicone, made for manhandling like Mansfield — no, this was the Satin Doll as Wonder of the World.

The only defect the studio could find in her was her height — publicity painted her as 'willowy — five feet five inches' but she was barely five feet tall. Her later weight struggles are explained somewhat by this; a tall woman can conceal a six-month pregnancy, but a small woman need only gain a few pounds to look fat. One director bitched, 'Elizabeth's face is her fortune — her body belongs to someone else.'

Her body was soon to belong to a succession of men. I shall not dwell on them: Nicky Hilton was a creep, Michael Wilding was a crush taken too far, Mike Todd was her equal, Eddie Fisher was a wimp, Richard Burton was a buffoon whose early sheen of brilliance was worn dull by drink and greed and disgust, John Warner was an attempt to grow old gracefully who lasted until Taylor realized that she wanted to *live*, not give dying a dry run. I won't dwell on them because the hurricane is the thing — do the news broadcasts describe in detail the individual units that the hurricane spins up, embraces and scatters as decimated debris? It is enough to say that Taylor's compulsive marrying was the most American thing about her; her hedonism, her generosity, her guts are very Europe. And very Brunette. Brunettes tend to break out of their beauty and win awards and the affection of women. Think of Ava Gardner, Sophia Loren, Natalie Wood. Blondes tend to wilt and wither. Since she was sixteen and the heroine's best friend and worst rival in *A Date With Judy*, Taylor had been a testimony to the perishability of the blonde. Wholesome Jane Powell became frail Eva Marie Saint became wispy Susannah York, and Taylor robbed them blind — their precious blonde hair meant nothing, it was just part of their doormat whole, something for Taylor to wipe her feet on.

Off the screen another blonde was running scared from Taylor: Marilyn Monroe. Monroe would go into a depression every time she saw a picture of Taylor, and mope — 'She has class, she has the Oscar, she has Monty. I got nothing.' Taylor held the record number of *Life* covers — thirteen; unlucky for some blondes. Monroe, her nearest rival, had six. Monroe was seven years older; she had no children, no fortune, no father. Marilyn made up to the camera, it was her daddy; Elizabeth cold-shouldered it. Marilyn ate and drank to blot things out; Elizabeth indulged to enjoy. Marilyn was *done to*; Elizabeth DID.

Whereas Marilyn struggled with the demons of the mind — which are often sadly no more than indulgences, interesting modern accessories; 'Let me tell you about my new trauma' say Americaines one has only known for

Taylor with Wilding and baby: she kept the baby

Taylor with Hilton: checking into Heart-break Hotel

Taylor with Fisher, the Coca Cola Kid: things didn't go better with him

two minutes the way a European girl would volunteer information about a new pair of shoes – Elizabeth Taylor overcame numerous terrible ailments. She had a heart attack at twenty-one, was on crutches with sciatica at twenty-three, suffered from appendicitis, a steel splinter in the eye, a twisted colon, three crushed discs in the spine and double pneumonia.

Now if there is one thing the female masses of the West love to do it is to cultivate an illness and complain about it to their friends, detailed to the point of drawing diagrams. They do it because they are unhappy with their lot but do not want to complain outright; this would hint too much at 'fanatical' feminism, would be 'unnatural' – though what could be more unnatural than glorying in illness, I do not know.

Elizabeth Taylor became a woman's woman – which the sex symbol must become if she does not want to retire at the sight of her first wrinkle – on the strength of her illnesses alone, although her weight problem helped a little. Monroe was not liked by women until she was safely sealed up in her tomb.

But perhaps the inferiority that Marilyn felt most insulted by was the difference in their status as working artists. The power of the studios lasted well into the Fifties, and stars who had signed contracts in the recent past were sore about what they saw as their exploitation; in their mind's eye they were infant chimney-sweeps, all because they made each film for a pre-ordained fee. The benefits of being a contract star – having vehicles bought and shaped and built around you – meant nothing to them when they heard about Audrey Hepburn. In 1956, her short-term contract finished, she took on an agent named Kurt Frings and commanded $350,000 – around four times the fee of Grace Kelly, a constant money-spinner who eventually had to be bought out of her contract like a soldier by Prince Rainier – for *War And Peace*.

Mr Frings, an Austrian, soon became notorious for the wads he could wangle out of studios on behalf of his select band of clients, who included Lucille Ball, Brigitte Bardot and soon Elizabeth Taylor. He has been called 'the man who killed Hollywood' because of the way he almost single-handedly shifted the balance of power from the studios to the stars. At the time the stars felt very righteous and rebellious about being paid properly, but in retrospect it was the worst thing that ever happened to entertainment – entertainment exists to make for a happy public, not happy stars, and the studio knew how. The balance of power has now moved to the director, who knows even less than the actor about what the public want and that is why people do not go to the cinema any more.

Still, Kurt Frings probably did not know where his talent would lead when he made Elizabeth Taylor the highest paid actress in the world by blagging half a million dollars for *Suddenly Last Summer*. And soon – the hurricane in the hands of the hustler! Too late to stop now! – there was a certain million-dollar fee for the costliest film ever made – *Cleopatra*.

On top of this, Elizabeth Taylor received three thousand dollars a week living expenses, two penthouses at the Dorchester, a Silver Cloud complete with driver and round trips for her husband, children, agent, animals and hairdresser, Sidney Guilaroff – borrowed from MGM at a cost of God knows how much.

Marilyn Monroe's last days were lived in the shadow of the Queen of the Nile. Fox was *her* studio and she was receiving a flat fee of $100,000 for her new film. She began to hold up *Something's Got To Give* when she heard that Taylor was holding up *Cleopatra* in England; she neglected the fact that Taylor was at death's door and had stopped breathing no less than four times while she, Marilyn, was simply suffering from pique.

The one sequence of the film that interested her and that she worked hard on was the swimming-pool romp. She peeled off her flesh-coloured swimsuit and frolicked, giving the delighted photographers their first nude shots of Marilyn Monroe for fourteen years. 'I'll be happy to see all those covers with me on them and no Liz,' said Marilyn, desperate to the last.

When she held up the film for the second time, Fox fired her. 'No studio can afford Monroe and *Cleopatra*.' They ditched their flesh-and-blood employee for a fictional exploiter; the hurricane, sweeping in and out of death four times, even now inadvertently made debris of an innocent by-stander. In the end, that was the one thing Marilyn could do better than Taylor – she could die.

Cleopatra cost fifty million dollars to make and needed to make back sixty-two million to break even, due to publicity costs. Of course, it did not, and from here on Elizabeth Taylor's energies went into her private life; Richard Burton acted as midwife, delivering Elizabeth to her proud parent, Mass Media. She had gained her freedom from the studio – the freedom to make bad films (some so awful they were shelved without showing), a free-dom she flexed to the full.

But it really couldn't matter less. Elizabeth Taylor has gone beyond box-office whim and now occupies her territory by divine right. Only she has grown old without becoming a parody of her screen self, a drag queen's revenge. She is a mass taste; the woman denounced by the Vatican and spat at by Americans provokes only admiration in the town where she was born – and, as everyone knows, where London leads, the world follows. When Elizabeth Taylor was due to open in the London stage production of *The Little Foxes*, a radio reporter went out on the streets to put the question, 'What do you think of Elizabeth Taylor?' – 'I've always admired her...she's got guts...she's not afraid of anybody' were typical answers.

I see her not as the Wife of Bath or the Queen of the Nile but as a female Henry VIII. Future generations will probably chant the names and fates of

Elizabeth contemplates taking a husband – but whose?

her husbands: 'Nicky Hilton, divorced; Michael Wilding, divorced; Mike Todd, died' and so on. Of course, she has shown much more mercy to her used consorts – but if she ever *did* have a yen to bring in the axeman...well, I am not sure she would not get away with it. Who dares stare into the violent violet eyes of the hurricane and say, 'No!'? A natural wonder; a natural catastrophe.

If she should die – and it is not at all certain now – Elizabeth Taylor's epitaph should read so: 'She was handed it all on a plate – and left none for Mr Manners.'

Chapter Thirteen
TWILIGHT OF THE GODDESSES

Shelley Winters — referring modestly to her younger self — has called a pretty face a passport. Rather, it is a *visa* — it runs out.

People are not kind to old film stars, they are monumentally cruel. In the film star, the immortal, decay reminds us of our own mortality, and we hate the bearer of the bare-faced truth. Men who loved the film star when both they and she were young, and could not have her, are glad to see her suffer; women, envious, are glad they have nothing to envy her for any more. The more combative of screen dreams fight time; Marlene Dietrich took injections of live cells to some success, while Mae West took an enema, weightlifted and washed in spring water every day to keep her amazingly beautiful skin just so. Both of these are policeman's daughters. Have hours of fun making up theories to explain this coincidence!

There are a few old standbys for the film star's last stand: the gauze over the camera, the big black scars behind the ears that eventually fade to shiny pink and signify a facelift. But most goddesses preferred cosmetic aid and to embalm themselves in alcohol, and I can understand it; your ordinary alcoholic is just a self-indulgent slob, but to be Rita Hayworth, say, to be *that* beautiful, and to look in the mirror one day and see that you are less beautiful than you were this time yesterday...you need some anaesthetic if you are condemned to spend the rest of your life watching perfection crumble to dust.

Some retire to marriage and some to animals; those that retire to animals seem happier, but those that mix animals with marriage seem the happiest of all — Kim Novak has a vet; Tippi Hedren has a wildlife conservationist, a Mr Griffiths, and shares her huge home with a colony of lions as seen in her documentary *Roar!*

Marriages to professional people who are definitely not in the arts seem

Dietrich: on her last legs – but *what* legs!

to work well; several ex-Chelsea Girls are spliced to teachers and academics – the silly film star gets an education and the dowdy swot gets a warm glow of glamour when his students turn up the next day and gape at him in silent awe because they saw the way his wife looks in a miniskirt in some old film on TV the night before. And the audience in a London theatre were surprised when a member of the cast collapsed and the old call went out, 'Is there a doctor in the house?' Up jumped none other than the fabulous señorita herself, Rita Moreno, waving her hands excitably and pointing at her handsome husband, who was, as it turned out, a master of his craft. (Starlets have lots of opportunities to meet doctors because they are always making passes at their wrists with razor blades and the doctors have to come round to stitch them up. It would be very romantic to think that Miss Moreno met her husband when she was hospitalized after the overdose she took when Marlon Brando foolishly refused to marry her – but this is probably my sentimental streak working overtime.)

Marriages that almost never work are those between actress and actor – all that ego grunting around over the ham and eggs every morning! In fact, on the whole it is true to say that the marriages of most screen actresses seem made in hell – most of them wisely keep working. If fame was small, the second career is easier – and of course the spur of financial need is a driving force.

Diane Baker and Helen Mack became producers. Dyan Cannon, Rita Gam, Mai Zetterling, Ida Lupino and Ann Todd became directors. Diane Cilento, Kay Walsh, Bessie Love, Yvonne Mitchell, René Ray and Françoise Rosay became novelists. Jane Frazee was a big noise in big business; Joan Leslie was a successful dress designer; Anna Sten's paintings pull the crowds to lots of exhibitions; lovely little Sylvia Sidney wrote a book about (of all the cute things) needlepoint; Susannah York writes for children;

Mai Zetterling in *Hell Is Sold Out*: her own films did not meet the same happy fate

Yvette Mimieux writes for TV.

Vilma Banky turned to golf; Eleanor Powell turned to God and became a minister; Eva Bartok became a hippie in Indonesia; Beulah Bondi travelled around the world twice – nice work if you can get it. Other resorts are Italian sex-and-scream films which will pay a famous face a fattish fee just to wander through the sick-flick in a Darvon daze; 'the stage', where the money is trash but the broken veins and broken beauty don't show; and the writing of autobiographies – these rarely fail to be touching. Even the hollowest star can tear at your hard heart with dead false fingernails as your eyes take in the decline and send out tears.

Just as many politicians are actors, many actors yearn to be politicians. Cleo Moore ran for Governor of Louisiana; Melina Mercouri is a Greek MP; Shirley Temple became a diplomat, while Penny 'Blondie' Singleton and the beautiful Gloria Stewart stuck to the Screen Actors Guild.

Kindness can creep out of the most vapid, vicious vamp as time goes by. Tallulah Bankhead's later days found her throwing many parties at which she would make a point of hugging her handful of leper friends in front of press photographers, in the hope of dispelling the myth that leprosy is

Shirley Temple: on the good ship Nixon

Shelley Winters: from status symbol starlet to proud possessor of said symbols

catchable by contact. Valerie Hobson lived for Lepra, the leprosy relief organization, in the dark days after the Profumo scandal. The B-movie cutie Marsha Hunt – not the black one but the blacklisted one – threw her considerable energies into black civil rights and the promotion of the United Nations.

The screen's loss can be the nightclub's gain; Rita Moreno, Cyd Charisse and Mitzi Gaynor – dancing girls, girls with skills – perfected stunning routines for ritzy floorshows. Occasionally the screen's loss was a nightclub nightmare of humiliation; the Sex Dolls Jayne Mansfield – who sat in men's laps – and Marilyn Maxwell – who did a singing striptease – both came to grief in dark, smoke-choked places, in their forties in the Sixties.

But how does a legend work nine to five? How does a legend *work*? Mostly, she doesn't. Garbo is alone. Gene Tierney is a recluse. Esther Williams will not be photographed in a swimsuit. Lana Turner confines her energies to lashing out at today's blondes: she found Jessica Lange in the remake of *The Postman Always Rings Twice* 'pornographic', while Tuesday Weld in *Madame X* 'had no heart-pull'. Ava Gardner is still a pirate. Hedy Lamarr took to shoplifting. Grace Kelly, who was every American house-wife's dream when she married into little league royalty, was busy until the day of her death with that most humdrum of housewifely concerns, way-ward children.

The ladies – Deborah Kerr, Loretta Young, Greer Garson and Olivia de Havilland – are well-preserved and popular. The gamines have grown old harshly; an old gamine is even less useful than an old Sex Doll.

Shelley Winters is amazingly sane and busy, but then she was shrewd enough to opt out of the Sex Doll stakes early and voluntarily and was actually a character actress by the age of twenty-five. Gina Lollobrigida has surprisingly become a good photographer and an occasional producer. Lucille Ball is a big power behind the scenes in TV. Marlene Dietrich still writes her own ticket: when making *Just A Gigolo* with David Bowie she refused to leave Paris for America and so was shot alone and spliced into the finished film. Lauren Bacall started so well in her second career as a Broadway star but became bitter when Raquel Welch – a hard-working and disillusioned actress trying hard to build a life around something more stable than silicone – won her part in *Woman Of The Year*, going so far as to strip the dressing room that she would hand over to Miss Welch of every-thing but the floorboards.

Sophia Loren, at the age of forty-eight, spent seventeen days in jail – in a pink prison cell, Jayne Mansfield's revenge! – for the crime of tax infringe-ment in her native Italy and the sin of greed. She says the days were 'hellish and shocking'; she claims to have been left with a heart murmur that will not go away. While she was imprisoned, her seventy-two-year-old hus-band, Carlo Ponti (marriages to Svengalis are not good deals, because a

Svengali always becomes a dependant), did not contact her once; he was no doubt busy promoting his new 'discovery', the Swedish model and songbird Madleen Kane, who I fear will turn out to be more Ekland than Garbo. Miss Loren herself is keeping company with a French gynaecologist; there is a cheap laugh in there somewhere but I am too disappointed in Sophia Loren's shoddy decline to crack jokes.

The only comfort is that Loren brought her downfall from Olympia on herself. There is no such loophole in Rita Hayworth's back pages. She never took a penny from any of her ex-husbands, not even the Aly Khan. She was sweet and beautiful. She was poor and she made herself rich. She worked hard for the War effort. At her peak – five foot five and eight stone eight – she made every other film star look like a doorstop. Yet she depended on the studio system to sustain her, and when it died she was done for, when there was so much left she could do.

Rita Hayworth once turned to her best friend, the stupendous screen-writer Virginia Van Upp, when yet another of her marriages was breaking up and blurted, 'It's your fault!'

'Why?'

'Because you wrote Gilda. And every man I've known has fallen in love with Gilda and wakened with me.'

The fault was not Miss Van Upp's, but a Hollywood unfit for Gildas, a Hollywood and an America so insecure that they could not let a woman, however beautiful, occupy stage centre anymore. Instead the screen was turned over to a succession of belly-aching brats whose only qualifications for movie stardom were male gender, bad tempers and an ability to keep audiences at bay.

Rita Hayworth lives in a beige and white four-room flat that looks down upon Hollywood. She goes out only to play golf. She says, 'I did what I had to do.' In 1981, at the age of sixty-two, suffering from pre-senility, she was placed in the care of her lawyer. She is Hollywood made flesh, in decay as she was in divinity. There has never been a generation of film stars so fortunate as the first generation, who placed themselves body and soul in the hands of the studios.

When a fan approached the retired Norma Talmadge, the ex-star said frankly, 'Get away dear. I don't need you any more.' Colleen Moore turned down four large offers of a comeback – imagine an actor of today refusing a comeback! – Hollywood offered, really too rich to bother. Corinne Griffith, paid off by her studio because her nasal drone drove audiences mad with the advent of sound, lives off the interest today. In the Sixties, Mae West turned down an Elvis Presley picture because she would not be allowed to write her own lines, as Paramount had learned it was wise to let her; Pal Joey suffered the same cold shoulder. She accepted Myra Breckin-ridge at the age of seventy-eight because she got top billing, the right to write her own lines and $350,000 for ten days' work – star-time all over again. And little Mary Pickford, under the eagle eye of her studio, formed United Artists with Chaplin and Fairbanks and was a multi-millionairess before she was thirty.

Behind every great girl was a studio. Those structures – a sort of extended Jewish family and remand home in one – practised positive discrimination before it was formally invented.

Studio heads assembled a stable of sirens that crossed the spectrum of ideals; these men were old, married and fiscal rather than physical. Because there was barely any fraternization between the studio head and the star (the starlet is a different matter – but then when the studios were working properly girls were only starlets for short periods; they either became stars and took power or dropped out and got married), actresses were not dropped when the boss became bored of his toy – the box-office was all, and actresses were placed in the hierarchy entirely on public reaction.

When Jean Arthur completed her Columbia contract in 1944 she ran through the streets of Hollywood shouting, 'I'm free! I'm free!' In her dissatisfaction with the films she had been allocated, it had obviously never crossed her mind that she might not be *worth* the studio's best vehicles. The fact that she was not exactly Public Love Object Number One and that Columbia had actually given her a glut of excellent roles along with the routine must have given her a rude awakening when she attempted to exercise her precious freedom. She made exactly two films after breaking free, even though she is still alive today.

Like teenagers who do not appreciate their mother until they leave home and have to live on marmalade sandwiches and Tizer, the actors who played up under the studio system were frozen with fear when they realized what a world without studios meant. The studios had taken care of business, of everything but the emoting. All an actor had to do was *act*. The studios crafted beautiful, unstoppable vehicles for them by employing legions of *writers*; Garson Kanin as opposed to grunts and curses.

It is largely the screenwriters who the goddesses have to thank for their immortality; the world will always welcome one-liners and the goddesses spat them like tickertape. It is amusing to note that Jean Harlow, playing Thirties empty-headed strumpets, displays more guts, wit and sheer memorable dialogue than any contemporary actress – take Jill Clayburgh, *please* – as an autonomous, sensitive, literate, modern woman. The only thing today's 'serious' actresses are allowed to display is flesh – they strip as reflex, whereas the little bits of fluff of the past could always keep a tight hold on their satin and tat. Stripping an actress is cheaper than getting a writer to give her some sharp lines, after all...

Harry Cohn, the nastiest of the studio heads, would prostrate himself to subterranean lengths to add an extra bit of talent to the Columbia roster. He said every day, 'I kiss the feet of talent.' His attitude demonstrated perfectly the greatness of the movie moguls; *they* did not consider themselves artists — they were merchant midwives, delivering the dreams to the people. He told George Stevens that he *knew* the director despised him, and he promised never to speak to Stevens if only the director would work for Columbia. To one writer he said, 'I'll do anything for you. You're crazy about a starlet? I'll let you take her down to Stage Eight and I'll stand outside and guard the door.' He was shameless in his pursuit of excellence.

He was procurer and protector. One musical star told Cohn that she was going to break her contract and marry a socialite. Cohn told her that her intended was a psychopath who had already, to his knowledge, beaten up at least two girls, burning one with a cigar and causing the other permanent brain damage. The star disregarded him -- disregarded a *Cohn*, a descendant of Aaron, brother of Moses! She retired to marriage, and when she was six months pregnant her better half threw her down a flight of stairs.

The studio system survived sound, the Depression and both World Wars — but it could not survive a ten-inch screen sitting smug in the corner of the room. In 1950 there were five million TV sets in the US; in 1951 a new factory town in Pennsylvania housed fifteen thousand television sets AND NO CINEMA. By 1960 there were *fifty* million TVs in America and cinema audiences were halved.

Hollywood took a sad revenge by making a string of films in which television was ridiculed, such as *Happy Anniversary* in which David Niven kicks in one set after another. Hollywood sadly fought back with bigger screens (CinemaScope, VistaVision) and gimmicks (3-D, Cinerama) and epics peopled with smaller-than-life characters in larger-than-life landscapes. Hollywood hung its head and gave up.

Actors, as ever useless without a script, chose this point to send in the agents, demanding huge fees *and* a percentage of the profits *and* script veto *and* a choice of directors. They were surprised to find themselves negotiating not with geriatric Jewish gentlemen but with cautious computers in business suits. The studio heads had been removed by stockholders or had departed in depression.

When Howard Hughes deserted RKO it was bought by Lucille Ball, who had once been fired there, and turned into a television lot. Gulf and Western Corporation bought Paramount, Warner Brothers now belonged to Kinney National Service Inc. The faceless ones prided themselves on being hard-headed, and analysed the ingredients of every proposed project down to the shade of the chorines' toenails. But it was this very hard-headedness which made them useless film moguls. The studio heads in their lion age had possessed a streak of sentimentality that had fused perfectly with that of the poor paying public to cement a perfect understanding of supply and demand of urban miracles, glycerine tears and happy endings.

Be bold, be bold, but not too bold! – the conceited directors who believed that the fall of the studio system would pave the way to a greater proportion of 'good' films should have heeded the word of Bluebeard. Instead, men like Huston and Kramer found themselves directly answerable to the conglomerates who financed them, so much so that if a production lost money it would be many moons before the producer-director could gather capital again. Thus the whole business of creation in the cinema became *ponderous*. No more one-week-one-picture à la MGM, employing and entertaining millions. Weighed down by the accountability their freedom had found them, they thought about every nuance for months, ignoring all instinct and inspiration.

Actors, ever opportunistic and addled, took advantage of this state of anarchic tedium. Accountants informed them that the American income tax laws made it advantageous for the highest paid of them to be corporations in their own right, producing their own vehicles. The Corporation Man in rebel's clothing!

Instead of taxable cash they could take home stock dividends, *pension benefits* (my incredulous italics) and corporate profits. This was the penny-pinching reality behind the freewheeling words.

So say hello to the new hordes of faceless hawkers with ugly names, crusaders for the right of every man to own a corporation of his own. There have been Batjac (John Wayne), Pennebaker (Marlon Brando), Jalem (Jack Lemmon), Bryna and Joel (both Kirk Douglas) and Cooga Mooga (Pat Boone). I'm sure these corporations will have made the cinema – not to mention the world – a better place to be.

Forget the villains of the piece – plush MGM, romping Paramount, gritty Warner Brothers, slick RKO, escapist Universal, sleazy Fox and opulent Columbia. Forget their character and polish and optimism and effort and panache and eagerness to please the people. Forget the studio days – or the days of freedom will leave you cold.

Forget the happy ending, which is gone for ever. The happy ending was the American equivalent of the stiff upper lip, easily tacked on to conceal the uncomfortable truth – that the British are excitable and emotional and that America does not contain many happy endings.

If time could be turned back and happy endings could be made to order I would like to tack one on to the end of the Sonja Henie story. Her twilight was a tearjerker to rival Sirk's best work. The sweet-faced Norwegian, who was the cinematic skating sensation of the Thirties, eventually contracted leukaemia and in 1969 boarded a plane to go home to Oslo to die. She was dead before the plane touched down.

Chapter Fourteen
LITTLE BIG MEN

Hollywood is not just a film industry, it is a barometer and a thermometer, it semaphores America's health. And right now it is making the most neurotic, depressive films it has ever made. It either wallows or it tries to escape – Vietnam or Venus. There are no celebrations.

To moan more meaningfully than man has moaned before is the American cinema's aim. As Hollywood strove to become 'real' it became narrow. How many people have fought in Vietnam? Robbed a bank? Become a vigilante? A boxer? Cinema left realism to go slumming, and it slummed its way right into a sexual ghetto.

'There ain't a thing that's wrong with any man here/That couldn't be cured by putting him near/A girly, womanly, female, feminine DAME!' sang the deliriously masculine chorus of *South Pacific*, and their advice to the addled could well apply to Hollywood in the last quarter of the twentieth century. From *Brief Encounter* to *Close Encounters Of The Third Kind* there has been a gradual *breeding out*, like a mongrel strain, of girls on film, and the result has been steady artistic and financial bankruptcy. In the Thirties, Mae West saved Paramount single-handed; in the Eighties, Michael Cimino – and no film fan even knows what he *looks* like – broke United Artists the same way with *Heaven's Gate*, which lost a striking forty-two million dollars.

I will call the drift *masculinism* (nothing at all to do with masculinity which comes naturally to all the best men). Masculinism can be confirmed through a handful of clues – homosexuality that dare not speak its name, going through the motions of genital heterosexuality but running quickly back to the boys when the dirty deed is done; a hatred of the present and a yearning to return to caveman/cowboy/Empire days; a hatred of overtly beautiful women and a reverence for dead ones; an obsession with things morbid, a desire to be a giver of death to make oneself the exact opposite of the woman, a giver of life. The masculinist can be identified because he is a man's hero, never a girl's heart-throb. He *kills*, therefore he *is*.

Masculinism started with Method. The Method Actor looked at the Sex Doll and thought her empty and unworthy; he turned to the mirror and the other man. In *East Of Eden* James Dean's love interest is Raymond Massey and in *Rebel Without A Cause* it is Sal Mineo – Julie Harris and Natalie Wood are beards who never get kissed.

Method actors came from professional families – Dean Senior was a dentist, Mr Brandeau (the original spelling – French (effeminate) not Italian (stallion)) was a theatrical, Mr Clift was loaded – and had rampant class guilt, which they attempted to exorcize in their patronizing parodies of low-life. Official Method ended with the deaths of Clift and Dean and the bulk of Brando, but the stink lingered on.

In the uncertain Sixties, Hollywood was shocked by the films of Sergio Leone, which starred an American resident in Italy – Clint Eastwood. These films, made from 1964 till 1967, made pots of money – largely because the outlay was so little – and were known as spaghetti westerns. They were dubbed and destructive. The central character of these films was less a man – no past, no name – than a machine built to work a gun, and Eastwood

Make my day – don't make any more films: Clint Eastwood

stopped making them as soon as he could afford to. Back in America he played psychopathic detectives who left their prey full of more holes than a second-hand dartboard. (Mr Leone went on to the US where he made *Once Upon A Time In America* which cost thirty million dollars and took three million.)

Although his audiences are laughably small compared to the late Forties' peak, Eastwood is probably the only actor working who can draw an audience to a cinema on the strength of his name alone. He even obtained a certain aged 'hip' following because his Italian films were thought to dish the dirt on the way the old West really was – of course, they were just another neurotic but new angle on the Big Wallow. These dupes were disappointed by Eastwood's film *Firefox*, a tired 'thriller' ('borer' would be more to the point) showcasing mindless Commie-baiting worthy of Joe Goebbels. I, of course, saw it from the first spaghetti-soaked bullet.

Eastwood himself is a corny character, standard parrot, curious only in the films he directs. They are coy little family-fun efforts, chimps and chumps running around having a smashing time – very likely guilt offerings to the general public who complain that there's no movie fit to take the children to see these days.

Hollywood caught up with the new western through the spaghetti spree, making *True Grit* and *The Wild Bunch* in 1969 – the western, symbol of all the slush the studio system had subjected sensitive thespians to! What a joke! Then there was another kind of cowboy – *Midnight Cowboy* – the forerunner of all the Just Good Buddies films to follow in which there was no leading lady but two leading men. The difference was that *Midnight Cowboy* – made by John Schlesinger, a 'woman's director' in the bravest and best sense, director of *Darling*, and son of Albion – showed exactly the sordid and senseless hole American men get into when they try to live up to their stereotypes.

The Seventies had the disaster film; the first and best, *The Poseidon Adventure*, was kept afloat by a brilliant female cast of ex-cuties and future beauties working as hard as they ever would – Shelley Winters, Stella Stevens, Carol Lynley, Pamela Sue Martin. The rest featured men running around being brave and bossy and busy.

Then there were the Noble Cop films – the only honest man (women were Worried Wives, trying to keep a good man down) in New York! The end of the Seventies saw the Vietnam crocodile tears and the spectre of war as spectacle.

The concept of entertainment is rather a sad one anyway – people filing into purpose-built buildings to be amused. Surely evolution did not mean to bring us to this point, this pointless passive point? Entertainment confirms that mankind does not know what to do with itself, that friends and family are boring, that like a big bloated pasha mankind will pay others

Marlboro Man at bay: Jon Voight in *Midnight Cowboy*

exorbitant sums to caper before him.

But if there must be entertainment, it should *be* entertaining. If one wants to know what war is like, one should look at the real thing shown nightly on the television news.

Men on leave in the Forties went to Rita Hayworth havens or musical extravaganzas because they *knew* what a man was – they knew what a war was, and they didn't want to wallow in it, just fight and finish it.

The masculinist doctrine holds that violence – one to one, one to five, massacre, war – is entertainment; this is its sickness and its suicide.

The steak on your plate, the plane crash on your front page, the fascist goon squad on your mind – death is there wherever you look for it, and now masculinist movie-makers have dragged it into places of entertainment. There is always a war somewhere, evergreen slaughter, and children burn as we banter and place bets on horses – yet death has been brought into our midst as a consumer durable.

'Experience *Apocalypse Now* and you will never have to go to war' said a radio commercial – men watch 'men's films' to see how 'real men' behave beyond situations of civilization, as if Clint and Sly and Coppola's Army were real men! They are mere artistics who find emoting somehow effeminate and so overcompensate with hysterical, pantomimed aggression, rather like poor old Norman Mailer, one of the first casualties of masculinism. These films are loud, loud lullabies to help scared, soft America sleep well. No sooner had *Rambo 2* (*Vietnam By Numbers For Retards*) hit the cinema than *The Delta Force* went into production in Israel, starring Lee Marvin and Chuck Norris as members of an American paramilitary squad storming the plane at Beirut airport to free the American hostages by force. 'We're going to change the facts and give people what they want,' said the producer happily, two months after the real event. As such, *Rambo* and his rivals are as perfectly natural as the films of Cecil B. DeMille and Depression Shirley Temple – yet more of America stumbling into the shit and coming out smelling of sugar, spice and everything nice. Do you really expect them to face the truth about themselves? Would you?

There is a place for the war film; but for the war film which shows war as hell, not as a hard man's heaven. There is all the room in the world for films about *bravery*; the three best war films ever made are about real people who seem a different species in that their bravery was as reflex as the brutality of the blue-collar buddies napalming 'Nam – *Odette* (Anna Neagle as Odette Churchill), *Carve Her Name With Pride* (Virginia McKenna as Violet Szazbo), and *Cast A Giant Shadow* (Kirk Douglas as Mickey Marcus). Perhaps the point is that Vietnam was *not* a war, it was one long atrocity – I realize that our American friends, living in a country built on genocide, may not appreciate the difference, so I will make allowances for them – and the miracle of Vietnam is that the massacred won the war.

Wouldn't *you* want to escape from reality if you were American? Fantasy has been one of the few growth industries in Hollywood in recent years. Escapist directors make films about dragons and knights, ghostbusters, gremlins and ghoulies, Conan and Superman, werewolves and elephant men and little green men, any kind of men but *women*. If women appear in fantasy films it is as breeding machines impregnated by actual machines – Julie Christie in *Demon Seed*, Sigourney Weaver in *Alien*. In *Superman* (Parts 1,2,3 and no doubt Part 66 by the time you read this), Lois Lane is allowed to look on in a spirited sort of way – phew, ain't progress wonderful?

The most successful director of the day (success meaning money, not talent or a place in the history books) is Steven Spielberg, always lost in space, whose film *E.T.* made three million dollars a day at one point. Spielberg's heroes, incidentally, are invariably little boys, clean and cute as hell, indicating a sick but refreshing dislike of *all* adults, not just female ones.

The masculinist crusade has a third front, and this one is the creepiest of all, selling itself on its singular sensitivity. It is home-front masculinism – the man as domestic martyr. Glorious old Hollywood held so many magnificent married couples but tired new Hollywood reeks of divorce.

One thinks with an involuntary raspberry of *The Champ* and *Kramer vs Kramer*; the woman is established as the villain from the word GO! because she walks out on her husband and child to 'do her own thing' (as if women never left because of perfectly real reasons like adultery and cruelty and utter boredom!) while the man is established as some kind of *saint* for doing the thankless daily tasks that women are born to. The men in these films cook Junior a baked bean – then hold out their hand for the Victoria Cross!

In *Shoot The Moon*, the most ambitious and aesthetically respectable of the divorce dirges – Albert Finney, Diane Keaton, Alan Parker, a roll-call to make the Horn of Cornucopia look like a Depression soup-queue! (I don't think) – the man is the one who ran, yet Keaton's wife (Faith! Why not go all the way and call her Faith Hope and Charity?) is such a dozy div that she makes the case for *him* five minutes after her first appearance. It is interesting that this tale of male desertion is the only one that the writer – one 'Bo' Goldman – admits is true, and interesting also that 'Bo' wrote *One Flew Over The Cuckoo's Nest*, a primal male whine in which women are either jailers or whores but all men are marvellously complex.

Marriage only occurs in American films when it is on the rocks, never as an ongoing situation (about the only thing over there that isn't). This is obviously a tenet of masculinist law; a man and a woman cannot live together – sexual apartheid. Thus marriage does not occur in modern American films as a backdrop to adventure but as a battleground, a forum for that most popular of American indoor sports – self-analysis.

American screen marriage owes less to Nick and Nora Charles than to Werner Erhard. Werner Erhard is an American dream and a universal joke; he was Jack Rosenberg, a used-car and encyclopaedia salesman until he read an *Esquire* article about 'great' Germans (a contradiction in terms, surely). In 1971 he completely made up something he called EST – Erhard Seminars Training, which means swine all if you disregard the Yankspeak – in San Francisco. EST weekends – in Britain they have been called 'instant enlightenment including VAT' — are run by 'trainers' who call dupes 'assholes' and 'refuse' to let them use the lavatory. Such abuse is said to improve energy, appearance and love-life but in fact is plain old religious scourging à la Opus Dei for people who think they are too hip to be religious.

Such transparent insanity could make a man a millionaire only in America: a country with an endless backlog of war crimes, and a populace who believe that their beloved country is too big a mess (a man living in an American city has less chance of dying from natural causes than an American GI in World War Two), too out of control to start cleaning up. They are probably right...but if only all that cash thrown away on EST could be given direct to the victims of America, the people that the guilt grows from...

EST is like the American screen marriage; the *solution* to the problem is not desired — the thing is to endlessly analyse, TO PROVE ONE EXISTS BY SHOUTING LOUD. The Me Generation happened when Americans realized that their country was not the world's policeman that Kennedy crowed about; their country was the world's vandal. The American whole was too horrific to contemplate, the American self became a refuge. And now they have made the cinema screen an analyst's couch.

They are hacks, these masculinists, and it has taken them a long time to hack their way up — no more Orson Welles boy geniuses of twenty-six in menopausal, movie-brat New Hollywood! — so by the time they 'make it' they are middle-aged and they make middle-aged films, either wanting to bathe in the blood of the young, like Elisabeth Bathory, in the belief that this will restore them to *their* youth; or to revert to wondrous kiddihood and natter with the Martians; or to break free of their jailer wife and pass themselves off as their ten-year-old son's slightly older brother.

Every title tells a story. The latest proof of a Hollywood on the run is the obscene addition of '2' or (for the classy) 'II' or even '3' to sequels of successful films. Where you find a numeral you find a film-maker terrified of never having another idea. Where you find a numeral you find a slur on everything the cinema ever stood for.

Another giveaway where artistic and financial bankruptcy walks hand in sweaty hand with masculinism; films were once called *Gilda* and *Jezebel* and *Roberta* and *Claudia* — at a pinch *Pat And Mike* or *Samson And Delilah*. Now we are plagued by *Willie And Phil, Melvin And Howard, Thunderbolt And Lightfoot, Butch And The Kid* — and they stink, all of them, of coy faggery and brazen vanity.

If *Gone With The Wind* was remade today, no doubt it would be called *Brett And Ashley* — or perhaps *Raging Rhett II*.

Damn damn damn damn damn damn damn — why can't a masculinist be more like a — Gable, Tracy, Fonda, Bogart — man?

Chapter Fifteen
THE BEAUTY
OF THE BEAST

Said Mae West, a while before she went up to see Him sometime, 'Anyone who has to use their body lacks something in their face.' How horribly right she was! Actresses from Mary Pickford to Marilyn will go down in the books as the greats, the goddesses, the immortals; today there is a new category into which practically every working movie actress will easily fit – The Forgettables.

Unforgettable girls do not tend to hanker after the cinema these days, they know that their beauty will be done down, rubbed in the dirt, used against them, resented by a director who is determined to build his film and his world around some mumbling male moron with a peachy posterior. They become crooners and star in three-minute videos that say more than four-hour bankrupting blockbusters can ever dream of; they become photographic models who can be sure that the camera loves them; they become TV actresses and are assured of their massive audience. They go where the spirit of Hollywood reigns in exile.

Because leading men are now so forgettable, actresses must be likewise. You see them as token X chromosome in all the best and biggest films (*Reds, Heaven's Gate, Ragtime*) with their soft, malleable, unpainted faces, the next best thing to a boy – glossily dowdy, translucent like a ghost, their talent is their ability never to attract the eye away from the MAN. Diane Keaton or Meryl Streep or Jessica Lange or Jill Clayburgh or Susan Sarandon or Sigourney Weaver or Elizabeth McGovern or Lisa Eichorn or Mary Steenburgen – all white, healthy, intelligent, American and more or less forgettable, passing through the memory bank like a dose of salts – not one heart-stopping sneer or show-stopping silhouette between them. Faces fit to launch a plastic duck.

You would think that a girl promoted and launched and financed by the

Diane Keaton: Little Orphan Annie Hall

Meryl Streep: plenty of nothing

last brace of sugar daddies in captivity would provide a dash of healthy, vulgar pizzazz – but Bo Derek looks like Linda Evans' shadow, and Pia Zadora looks as though she has escaped from a home for sulky midgets. When *Butterfly* was well into its salacious stride, and the public should have been slavering at the feet of their star, I noticed Pia Zadora posing for pictures in a busy city street while businessmen passed by with not a second glance at Zadora's lip-licking, tail-switching routine, saving their longing looks for the languid, leggy shopgirls and secretaries who made the Star look like an extra.

It took Europe to mop up the Gish slush with the lush work of Garbo and Dietrich, and the best big-screen faces are still from the civilized world. Marie-France Pisier and Isabelle Adjani are magnificent mugs frittered away on all that crying and preening and pouting that today's dull directors seem to consider the complete repertoire of the French girl. Nastassja Kinski, a maelstrom of a broad who acts like Louise Brooks off the leash; Maud Adams, the Swede with the swimming-pool eyes; Ava-esque Clio Goldsmith, uncovered and undiscovered in Italian films; and Lesley-Anne Down, a gorgeous glacier whose talent is eight-ninths submerged on the big screen as she attempts to hack out identities for characters so sketchy they should be played by skeletons. Goldsmith and Down are impeccably English, and English girls are popular in Hollywood – but only as

Nastassja Kinski: the face that launched a thousand turkeys

Sigourney Weaver: baskets, one presumes

symbols of submission, only when they completely erase their ability to talk properly and adopt Americanese. Jacqueline Bisset, Jenny Agutter, Jane Seymour and now unfortunately the chillingly beautiful Rachel Ward, who in the old days would have been honed by her studio to Hayworth dimensions but now with her new voice joins the ranks of the employed and the Forgettables.

The American film industry is protectionist to the point of paranoia, as all industries are when they are in the last stages of decline to dust, and two of the most beautiful faces of the early Seventies screen were cold-shouldered for the cardinal sin of Un-Americanism to clear a path for the dowdy divorcees next door who now rule the roost – the Jewish-French gypsy Maria Schneider, who retreated into lesbianism, and the English hourglass redhead Fiona Lewis who retreated into George Best (but briefly) and journalism.

Now Americaines swamp the screen, and very few of them are worth looking at. Of course there is Brooke Shields, a triumph of Italo-Irish co-operation; Goldie Hawn, whose resurgence and power has been a gorgeous shock; Margaux Hemingway who is a laughing-stock so far as acting ability is concerned and who has made me one because I think her acting is fine; Shelley Duvall, an elastic Giulia Masina and a dream to watch; Candy Clark and Theresa Russell, who effortlessly activate what Dean and Brando made so many ham-fisted passes at, acting from the depth of their bruises

Down among the dead men: Lesley-Anne Down, soon to be buried alive in ghost-town Hollywood

Rachel Ward: broken English

184

Liza Minnelli: if life is a cabaret, what was she doing at the Betty Ford clinic?

Catherine Deneuve: as cool (and suggestive) as a cucumber

and souvenirs without making a song and dance about it.

The demolition of the studio publicity machine and the sheer dearth of films made these days confirm Clark and Russell as no more than blank looks to the fan in the street – though Russell's association with Nicolas Roeg may make her yet. The stained old casting-couch has been shipped out and replaced by the ongoing meaningful relationship situation, and one sure way for a girl to get into a *lot* of films is to hook up with a name director/actor. Jill Ireland, Sondra Locke, Diane Keaton, Cybill Shepherd, Nancy Allen – one man's meat is another man's box-office poison, but these unspectacular little people are flogged to death by their fancy men and it doesn't take much talent to give a convincing portrayal of a parasite.

Now the studio, the shrine to the epic woman, is dead, actresses are treated like particles of dirt by their hirers and firers unless they have that big name branded on them. Liza Minnelli, Catherine Deneuve and Barbra Streisand were actually asked to *test* for the role of Evita Peron, *test*, as though the body of their work stretching back to the Sixties had never existed. They are asked to subject themselves in more ways than one; to create interest in their inferior product Jack Nicholson claimed to have had it away with Jessica Lange in *The Postman Always Rings Twice* while Bruce Dern made the same brag about Maud Adams and *Tattoo*; as if one cared about the conquests of these useless eunuchs! As if Russ Meyer's *Laura* never happened a decade or so ago! 'Her First Kiss' has become 'Her First Public Fuck' and so celluloid sex has become another spectator sport for the passive pasha-punters.

In recent years, the box-office black and blue and bust from the rampage of masculinism, there has been a clumsy groping back towards 'women's films' (which really means a film in which no one gets their head blown off in slow motion). Directors have feebly believed that they could re-create the popularity of the studio films by simply starring two women in one film – *Julia, The Turning Point, Rich And Famous* – Hollywood grudgingly saying okay, we'll let you girls be in films, just don't bother *us*, us boys are happy as we are. What a sad substitute such films turned out to be. In the studio days, beautiful girls helped each other *win* – now they sit around and moan about their failure.

A cleverer and more cowardly approach to recapturing the glory days of girls on film has been New Hollywood's rehashing of Old Hollywood. As if admitting that no one will ever want to make a film about *them*, Faye Dunaway plays at being Crawford, Marisa Berenson plays Leigh, Cheryl Ladd plays Seberg AND Kelly, Jill Clayburgh plays Lombard, Lynda Carter plays Hayworth. This is no Eighties panic – Carroll Baker played Jean Harlow in 1965 and Kim Novak played Jeanne Eagels in 1957, and both girls played fictional film stars based on their chosen goddesses/meal-tickets just to milk extra mileage, in *The Carpetbaggers* and *The Legend Of Lylah Clare*. Indeed, as soon as Hollywood's history was dead as desired, it tried to give it the kiss of life – *The Women* was remade in 1956 as *The Opposite Sex* (note how women was and is a dirty, frivolous word in post-studio American cinema!) with Joan Collins as Joan Crawford, June Allyson as Norma Shearer ad nauseam.

But influences are useless if you can't improve on them, if all you can do is drag them down to your level – perhaps that is the intention, to burn the books, hijack history, garrotte the goddesses. Modern directors, smelling the stagnancy of their rebellion, have tried to boost their box-office by remaking Thirties films peopled by a cast of a thousand hippies. Peter Bogdanovich, a man with wit enough to know that the past was best and that depression is the dowry of the post-studio director, has spent a good deal of his career trying to make films that would have been acceptable to a Thirties audience. His real weakness was the pomme of his peepers, Cybill Shepherd, who in *At Long Last Love*, huge shoulders bursting out of slinky Edith Head-ish gowns, or in *The Lady Vanishes*, replacing cool cameo beauty Margaret Lockwood and (aided and abetted by Elliott Gould) turning the elegant wagon-lit mystery into a group-therapy shouting session, blew the whistle on her beau's wishful thinking.

Faye Dunaway has annexed the old Margaret Lockwood role of *The Wicked Lady*, but the tightrope-walker tension in her face shows the strain of autonomy on actors, a breed who by their very definition need to be told what to do. Today's big-screen 'stars' have a surface toughness which comes from repeatedly hunting down a project, rustling up finance, staking out a percentage of the profits – leaving them with nothing left to throw at the screen, at the people. The soft, bruised centre that the true star must possess in order to addict an audience has been toughened up by the demands of the market-place.

Do we *pay* film actors to be fulfilled and autonomous beings? What looks best *up there* – one sad, studio-bound Monroe or twenty independent Dunaways? And who will be remembered? You would think that the Eighties' unearthing of the earthly delights of *film noir* would make actresses more memorable, but the angles are morbid – the stress is on *death* rather than *sex*, although the sex is paradoxically more explicit – and the girls – Jessica Lange, Kathleen Turner – are insipid *ingénues* who cannot even hold a cigarette with sass. In the archetypal revamp, *The Postman Always Rings Twice*, Jack Nicholson and Jessica Lange wander through the Depression in a cannabis haze. Whereas Turner and Garfield *looked* like sexy dumb hunks who'd kill anything that came between them, Nicholson and Lange, though at forty-nine and thirty-one loads older than the originals, look like a pair of skinny, vacuous hippies, the kind America has specialized in ever since poor bulbous Jayne Mansfield made them feel embarrassed about touting vulgar glamour.

One just can't imagine the hippie Frank and Cora getting 'uptight' about the 'hassle' of her marriage – they'd just smoke a 'joint', 'get it on' and 'split'. Looks maketh the love object; if not, Tatum O'Neal may as well star in a remake of *Camille* and we can all pretend that a thing of ugliness is a joy for ever.

Even Broadway cannot stop itself from poncing off hallowed Hollywood – two of the biggest hits in Broadway memory were *Applause (All About Eve)* and *Woman Of The Year*, Lauren Bacall rehashing the remains that Bette Davis and Katharine Hepburn spat out. And Garson Kanin, architect of numerous pearls which have fallen from the lacquered lips of the lost legends, adapted his memories for TV in the shape of *Moviola*, three passion plays recalling Garbo, Monroe and the search for Scarlett O'Hara.

But TV on the whole has bigger fantasies to fry. Conclusive proof that the public want girls – not *men*, not *machines* – on film can be found in the rise of the *soap opera* (pathetic masculinist term of abuse), which means drama concerning love and loss and other real-life stories, from daytime radio shoddiness sponsored by Procter and Gamble since 1939 to the most thriving and spendthrift art form in the world.

Everyone wants to be in a soap – Gerald Ford's son (*The Young And Restless*), Groucho Marx's nephew (*Days Of Our Lives*). And any actress who knows a swimming-pool from a soup-queue! Money, power, business and men are the backdrops and accessories of the contemporary soap opera, but the woman is the why and the wherefore. In the frothy opera the hand does not merely rock the cradle; it pulls the triggers that release heartbeats skipped and hatred sown. These characters, dismissed as dull kewpie dolls by cliché-ridden critics, are painfully real to their public, more real than all the blood, sweat and Method man-monsters of the big screen.

America's suicide rate goes up by more than five per cent whenever a soap character attempts suicide. Following Meg Mortimer's exit to Australia, British application for entry to that country went up by seventy per cent. And with the advent of *Dallas* — a vehicle for the roxiest, ritziest creatures since the gypsy in Ava Gardner's soul won out over the career girl, consumed hungrily all around the world, penetrating even the veil of the Gulf States — the domestic ratings ruler became a goldmine.

The soap opera is the *nouveau riche* relation of drama, vulgar and vital as all get out. The theatre is the penniless aristocrat, locked up and forgotten in the west wing, mumbling to itself nostalgically, and the cinema is the bankrupt millionaire living beyond his means. The soap opera has no grudge against the theatre and probably does not know of its existence, but the once supercilious cinema it has taken to taunting. The soap opera has become a head- or, rather, a face-hunter.

Dallas was built around actors the cinema had left on the side of its plate, and *Dynasty*, its successor, was built around Linda Evans, the missing link between Andress and Bo and the only protégée that John Derek had failed to interest the movies in. When *Dynasty* did medium-dull business in the ratings war, the creators asked themselves what they lacked and decided they lacked a big-screen star — an old-fashioned, studio-styled star. And as the American public didn't seem too thrilled by the well-scrubbed, sun-tanned spectacle of Linda Evans, they decided to go the whole hog and get a dark star, a European.

Sophia Loren was approached but, with an Oscar-owner's disdain,

Linda Evans: a girl built to kick sand in Schwarzenegger's face

Joan Collins: diva of soap opera

Linda Gray: the girl with the grease-gun lips

Charlene Tilton: neckless in Dallas

In her spare time, Victoria Principal – the good girl in *Dallas* – enjoys driving a) racing cars and b) men mad

turned down the chance to revive her sagging career and went on to make a film that became bankrupt halfway through. Joan Collins, built up and bulldozed more than once by the film industry, accepted. *Dynasty* rocketed to the top of the ratings.

Elizabeth Taylor has been hired for a few appearances as Collins' sister, while Laurence Olivier is wondering whether £2 million is a fair exchange for his artistic virtue – as though the old fool had not frolicked through big-screen trash like *The Betsy*! No matter – if Olivier wishes to remain a pure pearl beyond price, Peter O'Toole is lined up for the part. If the Swedish Sphinx ever changes her mind and returns to look a camera in the eye, by and by, a soap will be her chaperone.

The soap opera is the best thing to happen to the actress since George Cukor. A massive audience is assured. Facial flaws do not streak across your face like comets when the screen is so reduced. You will not be asked to take your clothes off. You will be paid for one episode what you would be paid for a whole film. Especially remarkable, and jarringly humane, is the fact that TV drama treats its female stars like a million dollars rather than a two-bit whore; not only does it not throw girls on the scrap-heap when they reach thirty, but Joan Collins was actually *fifty* when she dragged *Dynasty* through the winning-tape. Linda Evans at forty has a career and a cleavage so solid that her young usurper now looks like being the forgotten Mrs Derek.

Modern Screen and the other Hollywood comics abandoned the movies long ago and now the starry-eyed smiles packed in between the adverts for guns, fake ID and black magic revenge belong to the soap stars, the sitcom stars, the detective stars, the car chase stars – Linda Gray, Charlene Tilton, Victoria Principal, Pamela Sue Martin, Donna Dixon, Suzanne Somers, Loni Anderson, Priscilla Barnes, Valerie Bertinelli, Jaclyn Smith, Cheryl Ladd, Tanya Roberts, Heather Thomas, Donna Mills, Lynda Carter, Lindsay Wagner, Catherine Bach...they are blameless and endless and they are refreshing in that they do not need three hours' preparation with their coach in order to smile for the camera.

Some (Jaclyn Smith, Tanya Roberts) were models, too beautiful not to be seen living and breathing eventually; a lot (Gray, Mills, Principal, Wagner) are in their late thirties and have embraced TV with relief, having wasted their beauty in bit parts since they were simple, trusting Sixties starlets; others, the young ones, have grown up with an acceptance of the cinema as void and have gone straight into TV.

The older and plainer ones become greedy and conceited when they achieve a regular audience at last, ask for astronomical sums of money and leave in a huff when their whims are overruled. Thinking that their fans will follow them to the ends of the earth, they invariably set out to conquer the cinema screen and serve up such singularly unsuccessful films that the movies are no longer interested and television will not have them back. You can lead your fans to the ends of the earth, perhaps — it is altogether more difficult to lead them into a cinema.

Television is now so strong that it does weak little cinema the occasional favour — the ironically named *Fame* was a lame duck until a television series based on the film was made a few years later (the original cast on the whole refused to take up their characters for TV, they were so sure that all their possibilities had been drained), whereupon the original film was brought back to British cinemas by popular demand. The relative success of films with numbers after their titles (titles will soon be indistinguishable from licence plates) shows an audience desirous of the format established by soap opera — 'And next, *this* happened...' — and a film industry too frightened to refuse, and faces too forgettable to attempt the traditional chore of the film star — the working of miracles.

Leaders of their own fields like the crooner Deborah Harry and the mannequin Jerry Hall have expressed a wistful desire to become film stars — but where will they start? What will these fabulous faces do in the new Hollywood? Get swallowed by a big fish? Sit at home and knit and wait for the hero to quit romping with his buddy? Any girl who sets out to be a film star today needs her brain changed. Their literal loss of stature can be most mercilessly seen in the reassessment of the rights of the short hero; in the old days he had to stand on a box when he kissed the heroine, but today *she* stands in a trench. She has dug her grave and she must act in it.

Actresses can descend no further from the goddesses — in my mind they stand like the subjects of Soviet heroic realist posters, monuments to the glory of flesh and blood, the antithesis of the cold stone Statue of Liberty, the silent liar. There were never such great ambassadors as those girls — looking at them, one absolved America of anything, because how could such beauty have been raised in bad land? America let Europe feed on those faces until those girls retreated into death and madness and seclusion and the trance was broken and the truth appeared as the cinema-dark-blurred eyes began to clear — America was wound round us like a tourniquet, too tight to fight, talking about freedom.

As fear eats the United States alive and its behaviour becomes more and more unreasonable, people will gaze at the girls on film and sneer suspiciously, *'These* are the same people?' Yes — Harlow and Gable, Hepburn and Tracy, Bacall and Bogart were fairly representative of the way the Americans were. They had all the wit and charm and intelligence they needed, but they never felt *sure* and so they began to nurture brutality, an easy feature to perfect, as their national characteristic. But there were a few years — from the New Deal to the Cold War — when out of the beast came beauty, and it was impossible to tell them apart.

192